# Israel

## It's Complicated

With contributions from:
Deborah Bodin Cohen, Irit Eliav Levin, and Viva Sarah Press

**BEHRMAN HOUSE**

www.behrmanhouse.com

Some activities within this book include an optional, digital component.
To access these resources, visit: bhlink.me/israel, followed by the chapter number.
(For example, bhlink.me/israel5 will take you to the resources for chapter 5.)

## EDITORIAL CONSULTANTS:

Heather Erez, RJE, Director of Youth Education and Engagement at Temple Beth El of Boca Raton, Florida

Lesley Litman, EdD, Director of the Executive Master's Program in Jewish Education at HUC-JIR and consultant to the iCenter

Stacy Rosenthal, RJE, Director of the Haberkorn Religious School and Ma'ayan High School of Congregation Beth Israel in Scottsdale, Arizona

Rich Walter, Vice President of Curriculum and Outreach at the Center for Israel Education

Rabbi Laura Novak Winer, RJE, Director of Clinical Education at the Rhea Hirsch School of Education, HUC-JIR

Copyright © 2019 Behrman House
Millburn, NJ 07041
www.behrmanhouse.com
ISBN 978-0-87441-982-5

Library of Congress Cataloging-in-Publication Data

Names: Behrman House, Inc. | Cohen, Deborah Bodin, 1968- contributor. |
  Levin, Irit, contributor. | Press, Viva Sarah, contributor.
Title: Israel : it's complicated / by Behrman House staff ; with
  contributions from Deborah Bodin Cohen, Irit Levin, and Viva Sarah Press.
Description: Millburn, NJ : Behrman House Publisher, April 2019.
Identifiers: LCCN 2019000937 | ISBN 9780874419825
Subjects:  LCSH: Israel--Juvenile literature.
Classification: LCC DS126.5 .B3583 2019 | DDC 956.9405--dc23 LC record available at https://lccn.loc.gov/2019000937

Edited by: Ann D. Koffsky
Design by: Zahava Bogner
Printed in the United States of America

# Contents

# What IS Israel?

If someone asked you, "Where do you live?" you could probably summarize it pretty simply: "I live on Elm Street in Springfield, which is in the United States of America." And that would be that.

But with Israel...it's complicated. They say that what you see depends on where you stand. And that's true of Israel for sure. Almost everything about it—its borders, population, even its name—is often described differently by different groups of people.

## Design An Israeli Star

Fill the center of the star to the right with words that you associate with Israel. Write the words that you most strongly associate with Israel **larger**, and the other words **smaller**.

- Take a look at the words you chose. How many are positive words? How many are negative?

- What made you choose the words you did?

- Exchange stars with a friend. Which words do you have in common? Which are different?

- How different would the words be if you were filling in the star with words that describe the place you live?

## Its Name

Israel has had many names over the years. Here are just some of them:

## Write Your Words Here:

## 5. Israel

In 1948, the people of the newly formed modern state again chose to name the land after their biblical ancestor, Israel.

## 1. Canaan

During the time of Abraham and Sarah, the land was called Canaan.

## 4. Palestine

In 70 CE, the Romans conquered the Jewish nation and renamed the land Palestine.

## 2. The Land of Israel

After wandering in the desert for forty years, the Israelites conquered Canaan and named it the Land of Israel after their ancestor Jacob, also called Israel.

## 3. The Kingdoms of Judah and Israel

After King Solomon's reign, the nation split into two kingdoms: Judah and Israel.

# Where Is Israel? How Big Is It?

Israel is located in the Middle East. While it looms large on the world stage, it's small. REALLY small. You might even call it tiny.

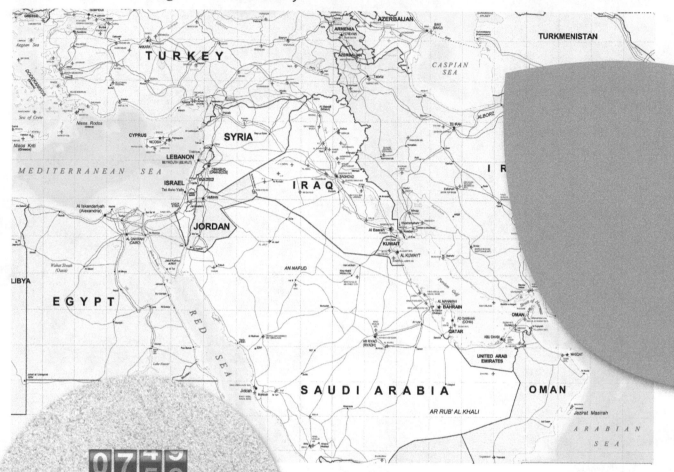

## By the Numbers:

Including the West Bank, Israel is 8,019 square miles. New Jersey is 8,723 square miles.

## Map It: Where's Israel?

- Use a pen or thin marker to fill in the area that is Israel.

- What do you notice about Israel's size now that you see it in relation to its neighbors?

- What else do you notice on the map? What do you wonder about?

Just because Israel is small doesn't mean it's unimportant. The land it occupies lay at the crossroads of the ancient world.

This made it strategically important, and it was fought over and ruled by one empire after another, including the Assyrians, Babylonians, Persians, Greeks, Romans, Byzantines, the Islamic Empire, Ottoman Turks, the British, and finally, the current nation of Israel.

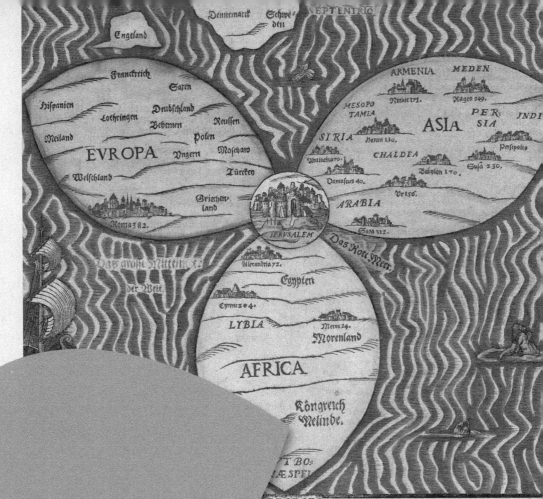

**The Cloverleaf Map** *by Heinrich Bünting, 1581*

## Map It: Create Your Own

With a friend, discuss the following questions:

1. What places do you recognize on the map above?

2. What places seem especially important from the map?

In the empty cloverleaf, create a map of the world today. What countries or continents will you include? What will you place at the center? Then, share your map with your partner, and explain why you made the choices you did.

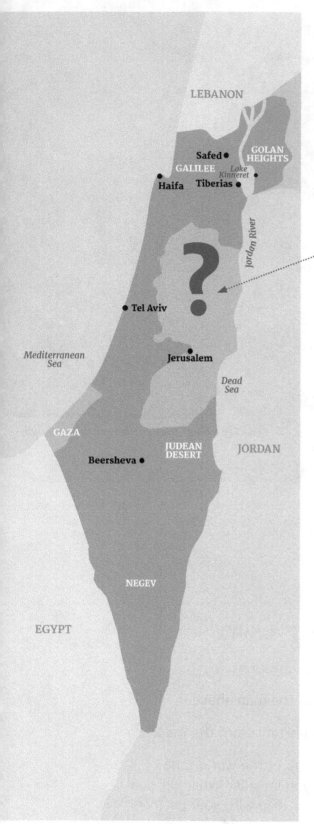

# What Land Does It Include?

Most of us can easily answer these two simple questions:

- What is the name of your neighborhood?

- What country do you live in?

But in Israel, if you ask those two questions about this piece of land…

…it's complicated. The answers will depend on whether you are Jewish or Muslim; European or American; religious or secular. Who you are, what your religion is, where you live, what your values are, and what your politics are will affect your answer.

The land marked with the "**?**" is called different things by different people, such as:

- Judea and Samaria

- the disputed territories

- the occupied territories

- the West Bank

For example, religious Zionists might believe that this piece of land rightfully belongs to the Jewish people and call it Judea and Samaria. However, Palestinians might call the area the Occupied Territories and feel that the land rightfully belongs to them.

The land itself borders the west bank of the Jordan River.

This book uses the names Israel and the West Bank.

# Gallery of Questions

Write down three questions you have about Israel in the space below. Then, form small groups, and share your questions with your group. Together, pick the three questions that you find most interesting. Write them on a piece of poster board or large piece of paper and post it to the wall.

## My questions about Israel:

Then, go around the room reading the questions. Add your own responses to them on sticky notes and stick them to the poster boards. Your responses can include:

- New questions you have that were inspired by the questions on the posters

- Ideas for possible answers

- One-word responses that describe how the questions make you feel (happy, angry, worried, proud, etc.)

Once everyone has posted their notes, walk around the room and read them. Then, come back and discuss:

1. What questions surprised you?

2. Were there any questions that you'd like to add to your own list? If so, add them to the box above.

3. How can you find answers to your questions as you use this book and learn about Israel?

# Chapter 1

# It's a Home for People from All Over the World

Have you ever been to a place where most of the people were Jewish? Your religious school or maybe a Hanukkah party? It probably doesn't happen to you that often, because in most places in the world, Jews are in the minority.

In Israel it's different. Israel is the only country in the world where a majority of the citizens are Jewish. Israel is also often called a "melting pot" of cultures—like the United States—because people come there from all over the world. When they move to Israel, they bring their traditions and languages along with them.

# What Do You See?

With a partner, look at the pictures of different Israelis on these pages and discuss the following questions:

- What do you notice about the people in the pictures?

- What would you guess about the people in the photos based on what they are wearing?

- Clothing gives us clues about people but can't tell us what they like or dislike, or what's important to them. If you had a chance to interview people shown in the photos on this page, what would you ask them about their lives?

Write your interview questions here:

# The Many Flavors of Your Community

Just like Israeli society is diverse, so is your own Jewish community. Stand in a circle with a group of friends. Imagine you are surrounding a giant salad bowl. One at a time, step into the bowl and sit down. As you do so, share what unique "flavor" you add to the community. You can share a unique tradition your family observes, or a special skill or talent you have.

*A home in Israel can be anything from an ancient stone house in Jerusalem to a high-rise apartment in Tel Aviv.*

# The Jewish Homeland

Where do you feel most at home? Is it your room? Maybe your yard or the playground? What about that space makes you feel at home?

Many Jews think of Israel as home, whether they live there or not. One reason is because of the Law of Return. It grants every Jew the right to move to Israel and become a citizen. If you are Jewish, no matter your age, or wealth, or your country of origin, you are always welcome.

## 0750

## By the Numbers:

A whopping 3.3 million Jewish people from over 100 countries have made *aliyah*—the Hebrew term for moving to Israel—since the founding of the state in 1948.

## Coming Home

Step 1:

Imagine you are writing a scene for a movie in which a character returns home after being away for a long time. Write the dialogue for that scene in the space below. What does the character see, feel, and hear? When you are done, trade scripts with a partner and review them. Then discuss the following questions:

- What did the scripts you and your partner wrote have in common? What was different?

- What emotions did the characters in both scripts feel?

My Script:

_____

_____

_____

_____

_____

_____

_____

*The Maccabeats*

### Step 2:

Watch the video of the Maccabeats singing "Home" at bhlink.me/israel1.

- What do you think the Maccabeats are feeling when they are in Israel? Why do you think they feel that way?

- What emotions do the Maccabeats share with the character in your script?

- Now that you've thought more about what home means, what does the idea of a Jewish homeland mean to you?

## What If You're Not Jewish?

The Law of Return applies only if you're Jewish or have a Jewish family member, such as a grandparent or spouse. Others can apply to become a permanent resident or citizen of Israel.

## Debate It!

Because Israel was founded as a Jewish state, it allows Jewish people, or those with a Jewish family member, to receive automatic citizenship. What do you think about Israel giving priority to Jews who wish to immigrate? Pick a side, and have a partner take the other side. Debate the issue. List the main points that you each made in the spaces below.

YES: It's a thoughtful policy.

_____

_____

NO: It's an unfair policy.

_____

_____

Which points made above do you agree with? Disagree with?

_____

_____

# The People Who Come

Jewish people from all around the world are drawn to Israel, and many have traveled far and overcome great obstacles to move there.

*American's making aliyah*

## Meet Karen

Karen is fifteen years old. She was born in Chicago, Illinois, and moved to Israel just last month with her family.

"My family believes that even though we loved our life in the United States, Israel is our homeland, and it's where we want to live."

Karen has lots of friends on her block who speak English, but at school, her classes are in Hebrew. "It is a bit embarrassing; I try to pay attention to what is being said, but everything is in Hebrew!" says Karen. "But I'm learning. I think by the end of the year I'll be able to understand Hebrew as if I grew up here."

## 07 / 50 By the Numbers:

In 1991, when the Soviet Union collapsed, over 1,000,000 Russians moved to Israel.

## Meet Roman

Roman, fourteen, was born in Israel. His parents and grandparents were all born in the Soviet Union, and the family moved to Israel in 1985.

At that time, the Soviet Union required anyone who wanted to leave to get government permission. Many who applied were refused; they were called "refuseniks" and considered traitors for wanting to move to Israel.

"My grandparents lost their jobs after they applied to leave. They wanted to live in Israel and be safe. Fortunately, many American Jews worked on their and other refuseniks' behalf. They marched and demonstrated. Finally, those efforts paid off. My grandparents got permission and were able to come here," says Roman.

"Even though I was born here in Israel, I speak Russian at home and Hebrew with friends. I am proud to be Russian, Jewish, and Israeli."

*An Israeli store that caters to Russian-speaking customers*

*Israeli and Russian passports*

15

*An Ethiopian synagogue in Israel*

*Ethiopian immigrants arriving in Israel*

## Meet Esther

Esther's family came to Israel from Ethiopia. "My grandparents say they can trace their Jewish family back hundreds of years," says Esther, fourteen.

In the 1980s, Israel rescued the Ethiopian Jewish community from the famine and persecution there by bringing them to Israel.

"My grandparents had a difficult journey. They had to walk with hundreds of others through a desert to a meeting place where airplanes took them to Israel. Not everyone survived—about four thousand people died on the journey," she says. "In Ethiopia, there wasn't much modern technology, and when my grandparents arrived here, they had a big shock. They had to learn how to use a refrigerator and other machines that they didn't have back in Ethiopia," says Esther.

"To me, being Israeli means sharing my Ethiopian culture with my friends."

07

## By the Numbers:

Between 1984 and 2006, about 74,000 Ethiopians immigrated to Israel.

# Meet Marc

Marc moved to Israel from France six months ago.

"My family and I loved our life in France," explains Marc, "but my parents were worried about the recent rise in anti-Semitism there. They wanted their children to be proud of their Jewish heritage and not have to hide their Judaism. I am happy that we came here," says Marc, fifteen.

At home, Marc's family speaks French. At school, Marc speaks Hebrew with his friends and teachers.

Marc's dad had a hard time finding work in Israel. He splits his time between France and Israel.

"My dad found it very difficult to learn Hebrew. So, he kept his job in France, and now he commutes back and forth. He tries to be in Israel every weekend with our family before he returns to work in Paris on Monday," says Marc.

"There are many people who work half-time in Europe and half-time in Israel. I sometimes wish my dad could find work in Israel and just stay here all the time. He loves his job and loves that we live in Israel," says Marc.

***Vintage French and Israeli postage stamps***

*Greeting new arrivals to Israel at the airport*

# Welcoming the New Arrivals

Israel has many programs that help immigrants become comfortable with their new country. For example, often the government gives new immigrants free services their first few years in Israel, including a free one-way flight to Israel, financial assistance, free health insurance, and free Hebrew classes called *ulpan*. People in Israel also create welcome packages for new immigrants, to help them feel at home.

# Welcome Packages

Pick one of the people that you met on pages 14 through 17, and create a list of what you would include in a care package to welcome them and their family to Israel. Then, draw pictures or make a collage of those items below.

Why did you choose each of the items?

_____

How do you imagine each item would help the family you selected feel welcome?

_____

## Who Is a Jew?

Can you imagine if someone asked you to prove who you are? That's the question that Jewish immigrants are asked when they move to Israel: Are you Jewish? And: Can you prove it?

Since the Law of Return only applies to Jews, you must be Jewish—and able to prove that you are Jewish—in order to take advantage of the law.

### But what makes someone Jewish?

This is where things get very, very complicated. Judaism is a thousands-year-old religion. Over the centuries, the worldwide Jewish community has developed a wide variety of religious perspectives. For example, some of the movements within North American Judaism—Reconstructionist, Reform, Conservative and Orthodox—all share core Jewish values but disagree on lots of things, even on what makes someone Jewish. The Reform definition is that anyone born to a Jewish father or Jewish mother and raised Jewish is a Jew. In contrast, the Orthodox definition is that only someone born to a Jewish mother is Jewish. Both traditions accept Jews by choice—people who convert to Judaism. However, some movements do not accept those who convert under differing traditions.

### What does the Jewish State do?

For immigration policy, the Law of Return accepts anyone who has a Jewish parent, grandparent, or spouse.

But: You still have to legally prove that your spouse or any of your parents or grandparents is Jewish if you want to make *aliyah* and become a citizen. This leads to complications.

For example, when Jews from Ethiopia immigrated to Israel, they had no way to prove their Jewish roots. Without proof, the Israeli government would not accept them as Jews and insisted that they convert.

While to the government this might have seemed like a practical solution, to many immigrants it was hurtful. Back in their country of origin they had to fight for their Jewish identity or were even persecuted for it. Now in Israel, where they thought they would be accepted as family—their word wasn't trusted!

In small groups, discuss:

* Do you think it makes sense for the Israeli government to have rules about proving Jewishness?

* Why or why not?

# Proving Jewishness

Split up into small groups and role-play. Choose one person to play a government official in Israel, and have the rest of the group play a family of immigrants hoping to make aliyah and become Israeli citizens under the Law of Return. The family members should decide which country they are from, how they are related to each other, and what their Jewish connections are. The government official should use the questions below as a guide to interview the family. The official can also ask any additional questions that he or she thinks could help prove Jewishness.

When you're done, complete the chart below to record the key points of the conversation.

| The questions were: | The family's answers: |
| --- | --- |
| Were any of your great-grandparents Jewish? If so, what evidence do you have? | |
| Do you have a document, like a bar or bat mitzvah certificate, that shows your ongoing Jewish practice? | |
| What objects do you have in your home that can prove your commitment to Jewish practice? | |
| Do you have a relationship with your community rabbi? Would your rabbi be willing to testify that your family is Jewish? | |
| The official also asked: | |

A passport stamp that issues its holder Israeli citizenship based on the Law of Return

## Talk about It!

1. Compare the different types of immigrant experiences that you learned about. In what ways were they similar? Different?

2. Which of the stories on pages 14 through 17 did you connect with the most? Why?

3. Why do you think people from around the world choose to immigrate to Israel?

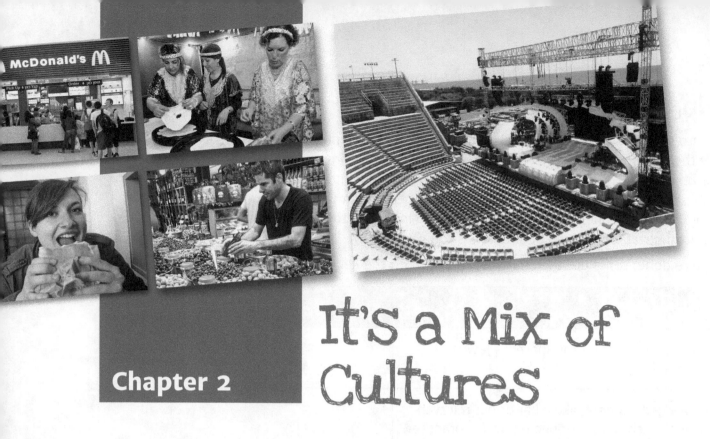

# Chapter 2

# It's a Mix of Cultures

In a school computer lab in Tel Aviv, a student clacks on the keyboard as she writes computer code. Meanwhile, in the two-thousand-year-old Roman amphitheater in Caesarea, fans fill the seats, waiting for an Israeli hip-hop group to perform. In homes, apartments, and even tents throughout the nation, Israelis nosh on foods inspired by places as far away as America and Africa, and as close as Iran and Iraq. Israeli culture is a vibrant mix of ancient and modern, Jewish, Arab, and Western—and so much more.

## What Do You See?

With a partner, look at the pictures on these pages and discuss:

1. What words or ideas come to mind when looking at these photos?

2. Several of the photos show examples of food. Why do you think food plays such an important role in culture?

# Jewish Culture

### Holidays

In Israel, how do you know a Jewish holiday is coming up? Go to the bakery!

Before Purim, lots of *hamantashen* will be on sale—chocolate, poppy seed, halvah, jelly—you name it. If it's Hanukkah time, donuts (*sufganiyot*). Rosh Hashanah? Apple-filled cakes and round challahs.

Like New Year's Day here, Jewish holidays such as Rosh Hashanah, Shavuot, and the first and last days of Passover are national holidays in Israel. Schools and most businesses close, and neighbors and friends greet each other by saying *chag samei'ach* (happy holidays).

## Compare: Holidays Here, Holidays There

Step 1: In the top box, draw or glue images that describe how you celebrate Jewish holidays in your neighborhood or synagogue.

Step 2: Then watch a video about how that holiday is celebrated in Israel at bhlink.me/israel2.

Step 3: In the second box, create an image that describes how Israelis celebrate that same Jewish holiday.

Step 4: Compare the two celebrations. What do they have in common? How are they different? What was surprising to you?

*Israeli graffiti*

## Hebrew

Do you ever speak Hebrew in religious school? In synagogue? In Israel, Hebrew is the official language. People use it in synagogue, but they also speak it in taxicabs, on the sports field, and when ordering pizza at a restaurant. Hebrew is everywhere.

## Heroes

Many famous people from the Bible and Jewish history are a big part of modern-day Israeli culture. If you are on your way to school, you might need to take a left at Rabbi Akiva Street and walk down King David Street.

*Israel's money—shekels—often has pictures of Jewish heroes, such as this one of Rachel Bluwstein, a writer and an early pioneer of modern Israel.*

# Design:
# Heroic Street Art

Watch a video at bhlink.me/israel2 to see a series of graffiti paintings from the Machane Yehuda street market in Jerusalem that brings Jewish heroes to life.

Then, print out and bring in a photo or artwork of one of the heroes that you saw depicted in the graffiti paintings, and paste it in the space below. Go online and find out five key facts about that person. Add your own words and drawings on top and around the image you printed to express your connections to this hero and how you feel about him or her.

# Arab Culture

About one-fifth of Israel's population is Arab, and they have a big influence on Israeli culture. Some Arabs are Christian, but most Arabs are Muslim.

## Arabic

"*Ahlan*. Are you *mabsoot*?"

That's Arabic mixed with English. You can hear that combination all over Jerusalem.

In Israel, many people use Arabic words within their Hebrew sentences too.

| Arabic Word | Used as Israeli Slang for: |
| --- | --- |
| ahlan | hey |
| achla | great |
| fadicha | an embarrassing moment |
| halas | enough, stop it |
| mabsoot | pleased with something |
| sababa | cool, I'm good with that, all right, fun |
| yalla | let's go |
| walla | wow |
| habibi | dude |

## Have a Chat

With a partner, imagine you are two Israeli friends meeting up for ice cream. Use some of the Arabic slang in your conversation.

Write the funniest sentences that you came up with in the speech bubbles.

*Kibbeh looks like a minifootball. It's made of meat wrapped in wheat and deep-fried.*

*Luna Abu Nassar performs rock songs in Hebrew and Arabic.*

## Music

Arabic music is also popular in Israel. Nasrin Kadri, an Arab woman, won first place on a popular Israeli talent show called *Eyal Golan Is Calling You*.

## Make Some Music

In small groups, choose a song you all like a lot. It can be one that you know, or one from a list of songs about Israel that you can listen to at bhlink.me/israel2. Develop movements that highlight the most important lyrics from the song. (For example, maybe the group stomps when an important word is said.) Perform your song and movement for the class.

Then, with your group, discuss the following questions:

- Have you ever connected with someone over a favorite song or band? Share why you think music might help bring people together.

- What can music tell you about a culture or community?

- How can music help people in minority communities share their culture with others?

## Foods

Israeli food also includes traditional Arab dishes.

*Knafeh is a cheese pastry soaked in sweet syrup.*

# Western Culture

No, we don't mean cowboys from the Wild West. "Western culture" is how people sometimes describe European and North American cultures. Do you enjoy soccer, shopping at the mall, or watching reality TV? Those are parts of Western culture. Many Israelis enjoy those things too.

## Sports

Israelis love soccer and basketball. You'll see Israelis wearing shirts, using beach towels, and sometimes even wearing *kippot* with their favorite team's logo on them.

Since it's very warm in Israel most of the year, beach sports are also big. There are plenty of opportunities for sailing, surfing, and swimming. Winter sports became popular in Israel when many Jews from Russia immigrated to Israel and brought their passion for hockey and ice-skating to their new home.

## Media

Are you a Harry Potter fan? *Star Wars*? Do you prefer Marvel movies or DC? There are Israelis who are part of these fandoms too. American, Canadian, and European movies, rock stars, and TV shows are very popular in Israel, and posters for movies about superheroes and Disney princesses—all in Hebrew—are a common sight in Israeli malls and movie theaters. Justin Bieber, Lady Gaga, and many more musical artists have all performed in Israel, to massive crowds.

# Design a T-Shirt

Do you recognize any of the things featured on the clothing here? Create your own T-shirt using Hebrew letters to highlight your favorite band, sports team, movie, or book.

0750

## By the Numbers:

Israeli athletes have won nine Olympic medals.

*Windsurfer Gal Fridman was the first Israeli Olympian to win a gold medal.*

29

# Ancient and Modern Culture

In Israel, it's common to see ancient structures that are thousands of years old next to modern skyscrapers.

## Israel Is Ancient

Do you like to go camping or hiking with friends? In Israel, many people do. And since Israel's history dates back more than thirty-five hundred years, visitors to Israel often like to go to one of the hundreds of archaeological sites that can be found throughout the country.

In fact, there's so much history that sometimes people stumble across it by accident! For example, in 2018, school kids digging a new walking path for the Sanhedrin Trail in the Galilee stumbled upon a fourteen-hundred-year-old oil lamp and a rare, ancient gold coin.

*"As I was walking I was looking at the ground; I saw something gold. I saw it was some kind of coin with Arabic writing. I brought it to one of the archaeologists. I thought it was something ancient, but not to this extent."*

—**Ilai Yonah,** high school student

## Israel Is Modern

Everyday life in Israel is modern. People commute on buses and trains; they go to work and school; they use banks and electricity, talk on smart phones—all the regular conveniences of modern life.

## Design a Modern and Ancient Show

Watch a video from the Jerusalem Festival of Light at bhlink.me/israel2. Then, imagine you had the chance to create your own light show, highlighting Israel's unique culture.
What modern symbols would you include?
What ancient ones?
Draw or paste pictures of them onto the bricks on this page.

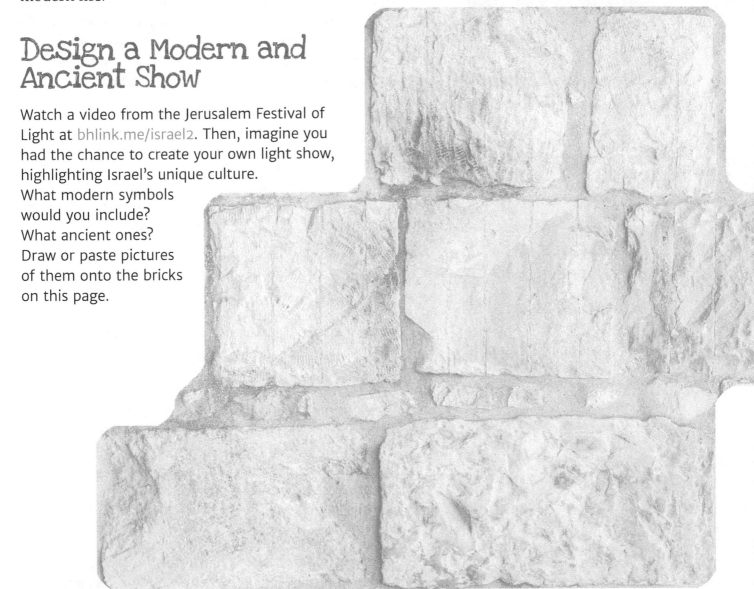

# Diverse or Divided? Or Both?

People from many places, backgrounds, and walks of life come together each day in every corner of Israel. You might take a bus that's driven by a Christian Arab, pick up a snack at a shop owned by a religious Muslim, and sit down at your desk at school next to an Ethiopian Jew. Most of the time, people get along.

*Pop duo Static & Ben-El Tavori.*

## It's Diverse

Israeli culture is chock-full of diverse influences. The pop duo Static & Ben-El Tavori mix a little bit of everything into their songs: rap beats, Brazilian styles, Japanese tunes, and Hebrew pop. *Ajami*, an Israeli film that was nominated for an Academy Award in 2010, features both Arab and Jewish characters. Hungry? In Israel, you can choose to have anything from an American-style hamburger to a Middle Eastern falafel with hummus.

## It's Divided

*Teachers and students from Hand in Hand, an organization that matches Arab and Jewish schools and has them join together for fun activities.*

Some Israelis choose to live in communities only with people who share their unique backgrounds and specific values, separate from other parts of Israeli society. And so, despite all this diversity, Israeli culture can be quite divided.

For example, many ultra-Orthodox Jews choose to live in neighborhoods where no one drives on Shabbat, and many secular Jews want a place where movies and nightlife are available on Friday nights. Muslim families might like a home near Arabic-speaking neighbors and a mosque, while a lawyer from England might want a modern apartment with other English speakers nearby.

Schools are also divided. Israeli families choose which schools to attend, and there are many options: there are different schools for secular Jews, religious Jews, and Arabs. There are religiously focused schools that emphasize Jewish subjects. Some of these are Orthodox yeshivas, in which students study Torah intensively. Others, like the TALI schools, emphasize both secular and Jewish studies.

There are also schools that are deliberately multicultural, where classes are taught in both Hebrew and Arabic, and students and teachers come from diverse backgrounds.

# Debate It!

Oren is an Israeli trying to decide where to go to high school. He's always gone to a TALI school, where he's had lots of Jewish friends and enjoyed learning Jewish subjects, like Jewish holidays and the history of Zionism. But now he is wondering if he should go to a multicultural school, where he'll learn less about Judaism but get to meet students from Arab backgrounds.

Should Oren go to a Jewish school or a multicultural school? Pair up with a friend and debate the issue. Have one of you argue each side. List the main points that you each make in the spaces below.

Oren should go to a Jewish school:

_____

_____

Oren should go to a multicultural school:

_____

_____

Which type of school would you want to attend if you lived in Israel?

_____

_____

Why?

_____

## Talk about It!

1. Think about your own community. What are some of the good things that come from diversity? What are some of the challenges?

2. What is the single most important thing you know about Israeli culture? What makes it so important to you?

3. Imagine living in Israel for a year. What parts of Israeli culture would you most look forward to experiencing?

Abraham's Journey from Ur to Canaan *by József Molnár, 1850*

**Chapter 3**

# It's Religious

Can you remember when you first learned about Israel? Did you hear about it at Hebrew school or synagogue? Have you always thought of Israel as a Jewish place?

Israel certainly has many Jewish connections. But it is also sacred to Christianity, Islam, and other religions too.

*In the Torah, God says to Abraham: "Go forth from your native land and from your father's house to the land that I will show you. I will make of you a great nation, and I will bless you; I will make your name great, and you shall be a blessing."*

**—Genesis 12:1-2**

# The Jewish Connection

Judaism has always been connected to the land of Israel, starting with Abraham and Sarah, the very first Jews. In the Bible they are told by God to go to a "place that I will show you." In an act of pure faith, they packed their belongings and moved to that new place—the land of Israel. Years later, Moses leads the Israelites through the desert toward the land of Israel. And later, King Solomon built the first of the two Holy Temples in Israel, where Jews prayed and served God.

*Worshippers at the Western Wall, the Church of the Holy Sepulchre, and the Dome of the Rock*

# A Lech L'cha Text Study and Song

Listen to Debbie Friedman's Song "L'Chi Lach" at bhlink.me/israel3. With a partner, discuss the following questions:

1. Compare Debbie Friedman's song with the Torah's text on page 34. How are they similar? Different?

2. Imagine you received the same message. How would you feel about moving to a new land, especially one that you knew almost nothing about?

3. In groups of three or four, create a skit in which Abraham and Sarah discuss whether to accept God's commandment to go to a new land. What concerns might they have? What might Abraham and Sarah be excited about? Nervous about? Share your skit with the class.

Lech L'cha Script:

_____

_____

_____

_____

_____

_____

_____

## What Do You See?

With a partner, look at the images on these pages. Then discuss:

- What do the images have in common? How are they different?

- What do you see in the photos that tells you something religious is happening?

35

*A carving from the Arch of Titus showing the Roman army carrying away the Temple's Menorah*

## The Kotel

The Jewish people's yearning for their homeland was also expressed in their connection to Judaism's holiest site, called the Kotel or Western Wall. The Kotel is one of the walls that surrounded the Second Temple. Jews come from all over the world to pray there, and many believe that God will answer prayers that are written on slips of paper placed between the stones of the Wall.

You can even send a message online and volunteers will place a physical copy of your note in the Kotel for you. Visit bhlink. me/israel3 to learn how.

## Temple Times

For hundreds of years, Jewish life was centered around the ancient Temple in Jerusalem. People celebrated holidays, came to see friends and family, conducted business, and worshipped God. But in the year 70 CE, the Romans invaded Israel, destroyed the Second Temple, and forced most of the Jews to leave.

The Jews were devastated. For years, their lives and religion had been centered around the land of Israel. What would they do now? Yet, they eventually built a religion that could survive and thrive outside the land, without the Temple. They created synagogues, places of learning and worship, and new holiday traditions.

*Women praying at the Kotel in the 1800s and today*

## From Temple to Today

But even as the Jews built new lives, they carried their connection to the land of Israel in their hearts. In every generation they created songs, prayers, and art that embodied their deep yearning for their homeland.

## 07 By the Numbers:

About 11,000,000 people visit the Kotel each year.

# Text Study: Connections to Israel

*Dan Nichols*

In small groups, read the poem below, then listen to the songs by Dan Nichols and the Fountainheads at bhlink.me/israel3.

## My Heart Is in the East

*My heart is in the east, and I in the uttermost west—*

*How can I find savor in food? How shall it be sweet to me?*

*How shall I render my vows and my bonds, while yet*

*Zion lieth beneath the fetter of Edom, and I in Arab chains?*

—by Yehudah Halevi, 1075–1141

- Discuss: What do the modern songs have in common with Yehudah Halevi's ancient poem? What themes do they share?

- In the sheet music below, write the emotions each artist expresses.

- In the last row, describe how listening to their words made you feel.

*The Fountainheads*

Yehudah Halevi

Dan Nichols

The Fountainheads

Me

# Religious Connections

## The Muslim Connection

One of the most recognizable buildings in Jerusalem is the Dome of the Rock (right). Islam teaches that it is the place from which the prophet Muhammad ascended to heaven. Next door to the Dome of the Rock is the Al-Aqsa Mosque. Together, they represent Islam's third holiest site in the world.

## The Christian Connection

Jesus of Nazareth, whom many Christians refer to as the Son of God, was born, lived, and died in the land of Israel. Many Christians visit Israel and walk the Via Dolorosa, the path that Jesus walked on the way to his crucifixion. The path ends at the Church of the Holy Sepulchre (left), which is considered one of the holiest churches in the world.

*The Druze community considers Jethro, the father-in-law of Moses, to be one of their most important prophets. Jethro's tomb, in Tiberias called the tomb of Nabi Shu'ayb, is a site sacred to their community.*

*Located in Haifa, the Baha'i Gardens are the world center of the Baha'i faith. They include the tomb of the Báb, the founding prophet of the Baha'i religion.*

# What Do You See?

Look at the image to the right. What do you see?
Write your answer here:

_____

_____

Now look at the picture again. On second glance,
do you see it differently?

_____

_____

Discuss the following questions with a partner:

1. How did your thinking about the picture change after you
   realized that there was more than one way to see it?

2. People from many faiths—Jews, Christians, Muslims,
   and others—come to visit Jerusalem. In what ways do you
   think they might see Jerusalem similarly? Differently?

3. In what ways did learning that Jerusalem means
   different things to people of different faiths
   change your own understanding of Jerusalem?

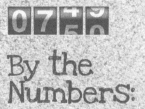

## By the Numbers:

In Jerusalem there
are more than 1,000
synagogues, 150 churches,
and 70 mosques.

# Are Sacred Spaces Shared?

**S**acred sites in Israel are sometimes considered holy by more than one religion, and compromises are often made when groups share access to holy sites.

## Sharing The Temple Mount

Perhaps the most revered—and contested—place on earth is the Temple Mount, an plaza directly above the Western Wall.

In 1967, Israel captured Jerusalem, including the Temple Mount, from Jordan. After nearly two thousand years, Jews controlled the site of their ancient Temple. Israel agreed to share control of the Temple Mount. Muslim authorities would govern all activities on the Temple Mount, and Jewish authorities would control the entrances leading to it.

## Sharing the Church of the Holy Sepulchre

A quarter mile from the Temple Mount, Christian pilgrims flock to the Church of the Holy Sepulchre. Six different Christian sects share control of it: Catholic, Greek Orthodox, Armenian Apostolic, Syriac Orthodox, Ethiopian, and Coptic.

These groups follow guidelines for sharing the space established centuries ago. To keep ownership of the site neutral, church officials have entrusted the same Muslim family with the church's keys for the past nine hundred years.

## Does Sharing Work?

Every day Muslims, Jews, and Christians work together to ensure that everyone has access to Jerusalem's holy spaces, and every day thousands of people visit them.

But sometimes there's conflict. For example, in 2002, an Egyptian monk was guarding the Coptic space at the Church of the Holy Sepulchre. He chose to move his chair to a shadier spot. But that shady spot was in the Ethiopian Christian area. The ensuing fight sent eleven monks to the hospital.

Another time, Israelis tried to install metal detectors at the entrances to the Temple Mount. Muslims were outraged, fearing that Israel was making a change to the long-held agreement. Israel removed the metal detectors within weeks.

Within the densely populated Old City of Jerusalem, sharing is essential but also complicated.

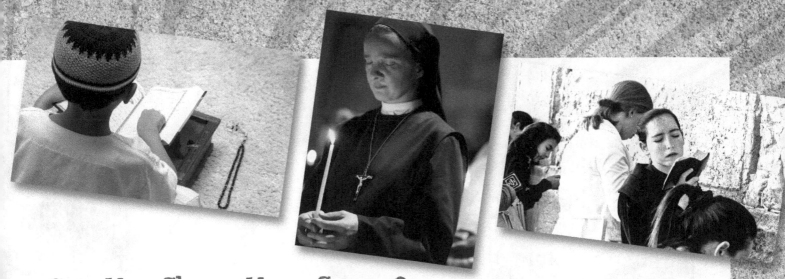

# Can You Share Your Space?

Break up into groups of three or four. On separate pieces of paper, each of you make your own collage about a place that is important to you. It can be your room, a favorite vacation spot, or any place that has meaning for you. But, as a group, you only get one glue stick or roll of tape, one pair of scissors, and just two markers. After five minutes, you can add more supplies.

When your collages are done, discuss with your group:

1. How did it feel to have to share the supplies for your project?

2. What might have happened if one of you had refused to share one of the supplies?

3. What if, instead of simple art supplies, the things you were asked to share were important to you? How would it have felt to share your most prized possession?

## Talk about It!

1. Describe an emotional connection that you have to a place. It could be a building, like your home or school, or something smaller, like the corner of your room.

2. If you traveled to Israel, which of the holy sites would you like to visit? Would you want to visit one that is sacred to a religion other than your own?

3. How do you think you might feel on your visit? How might those feelings be similar to or different from your feelings when you visit the spot you described in the first question?

*"For me, the source of coexistence for Islamic and Christian religions is the Church of the Holy Sepulchre."*

—**Adeeb Joudeh**, current keeper of the keys

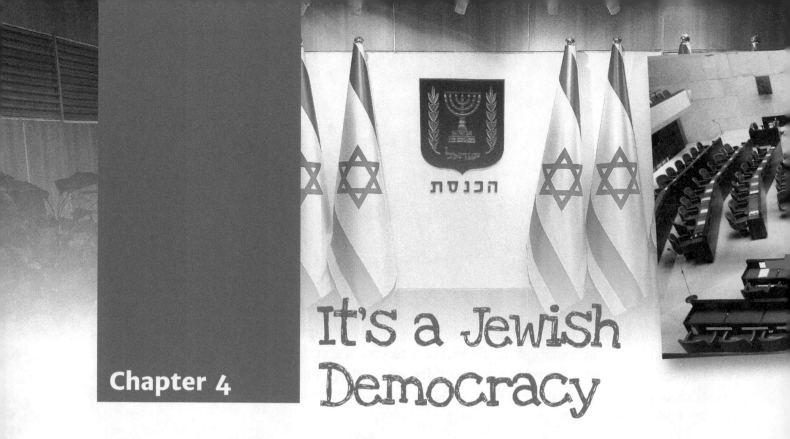

# Chapter 4

# It's a Jewish Democracy

Ever have a Reese's Peanut Butter Cup and enjoyed how the chocolate mixes with the peanut butter? Israel's government is sort of like that. But instead of chocolate mixing with peanut butter, democracy gets tangled up with Judaism—and vice versa. Unlike the United States, in which there is a strict separation of church and state, there's no official separation of religion from government in Israel, and the political system in Israel contains elements of two different systems: democracy and Judaism.

*"The State of Israel will...be based on freedom, justice and peace as envisaged by the prophets of Israel; it will ensure complete equality of social and political rights to all its inhabitants irrespective of religion, race or sex; it will guarantee freedom of religion, conscience, language, education and culture; it will safeguard the Holy Places of all religions...."*

—Excerpt from **Israel's Declaration of Independence**

## It's a Democratic State

All of Israel's citizens enjoy certain rights no matter which religion they follow (or don't follow), the color of their skin, or their gender. Every citizen of Israel has freedom of religion and freedom of speech, and can vote and run for elected office (when they are old enough).

These freedoms have allowed people from all backgrounds, religions, and genders to contribute and be successful in Israel. Government leaders, heads of businesses, and top military officers have included people who are Jewish, Muslim, Christian, Druze, black, white, male, and female.

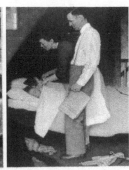

**Freedom of Speech, Freedom of Worship, Freedom from Want,** *and* **Freedom from Fear,** *by Norman Rockwell, 1943*

# Freedom Poster for Israel

Pick one of Rockwell's paintings above. Reimagine it by illustrating the same concept using Israeli (not American) imagery and modern symbols (instead of those from the 1940s). Create your final poster on a poster board, using markers, paints, or collage techniques. Then fill out the artist statement below:

## MY ARTIST STATEMENT

I chose to reimagine Rockwell's poster about:

_____

The title for my piece is:

_____

I chose to use these symbols:

_____

because:

_____

# What Do You See?

With a partner, take a look at how the chairs are arranged in this room, the main chamber of the Knesset, Israel's legislature. It was designed to look like a menorah. Do you see it?

Discuss with your partner:

- Why might the people designing this room have used that shape?

- In addition to the menorah shape, the chairs are also set up so people can see one another and easily talk. What values do you think led to that decision?

*The Knesset building*

> "We are not a Jewish state with democratic values; we are not a democracy with Jewish values. We are a state which has both Jewish and democratic values.
>
> —**Aharon Barak,** former president of Israel's Supreme Court

# The Knesset

The Knesset is the legislative (lawmaking) branch of the Israeli government, much like the US Congress. But there is an important difference: In the US, you vote for a candidate. In Israel, people vote for political parties.

For example, Likud is a large party that is politically right-wing; Labor is politically left-wing; Shas primarily represents Sephardic, ultra-Orthodox Jews; and Wamab represents Arab voters.

If a party gets a certain number of votes, they are represented in the government. The number of representatives they have in the Knesset is proportional to the number of votes their party receives.

*Israel's democratic values have allowed its LGBTQ community to grow into the strongest and most open in the Middle East. Each year there are pride parades in Israeli cities.*

*Two Knesset members from different parties arguing*

## Disagreement at the Knesset

Because Knesset members represent many different political parties and viewpoints, they often debate issues and try to convince one another of their positions. Parties often choose to work together in order to get things done.

For example, the right-wing Likud party might agree to help the ultra-Orthodox Shas party gain funding for ultra-Orthodox schools; in exchange Shas might choose to support Likud's position on the peace process.

# Do You Disagree?

Hang up two signs on opposite walls of the room: "Agree" and "Disagree." Ask someone to read the statements below out loud.

The statements:

- I want to visit Israel as soon as possible.

- Israel is a Jewish country.

- Israel is a diverse country.

- Praying at the Kotel would be meaningful to me.

After each statement is read, stand near the sign that best describes your feelings about that statement. Stand closer to the sign if you feel strongly, and further away to it if you feel less strongly.

Then, ask the individuals closest to each sign to explain their position on the subject. After everyone has heard those two explanations, they can choose to reposition themselves in relationship to the signs.

Afterward, discuss the questions below:

1. How did it feel when you heard opinions different than your own?

2. Did any of the arguments made convince you to reposition yourself? If so, why? If not, why not?

3. Which statement got the largest range of responses? In what ways did that affect your own ideas about the statement?

4. How do you think having debate and disagreement within the Knesset might be helpful for Israel's government? How might it be harmful?

# It's a Jewish State

The Israeli army is required by law to serve kosher food to its soldiers. On Shabbat, Israeli government offices close and buses stop running. Israel's official language is Hebrew, its flag displays the Jewish star, and its official seal displays the Menorah. Israel is a Jewish country—no doubt about it.

## Which Kind of Jewish?

*A restaurant's kosher certification*

Israeli Jews may identify themselves as Orthodox, traditional, Reform, liberal, Conservative, or secular—and those are just some of the choices. Each has its own perspective of what it means to live Jewishly.

Despite that diversity, the laws that regulate Jewish practice in Israel are under Orthodox control.

When leaders were trying to establish the state, David Ben-Gurion, who became Israel's first prime minister, wanted to secure the support of the Orthodox. He approached the largest Orthodox group, and together they agreed that in exchange for Orthodox support, parts of Israeli society—such as marriage, divorce, the legal definitions of kosher and Shabbat—would fall under the control of Orthodox authorities. They also agreed that Orthodox men who were full-time yeshiva students would not be required to serve in the army.

As a result of that long-ago agreement, today's laws in Israel often seem tailored for Orthodox Jews and alienating to the non-Orthodox.

## Q&A

Have three people choose one of the characters below, and perform the script on page 47.

**Sarah:**
a secular Jew

**Mosheh:**
an ultra-Orthodox Jew

**Ya'akov:**
the host of a local news podcast

## TOUGH QUESTIONS WITH YA'AKOV

**Ya'akov:** Welcome. We're here to talk about the religious laws in Israel.

**Sarah:** Thank you for having us.

**Mosheh:** It's a pleasure to be here.

**Ya'akov:** Mosheh, I'll start with you. Do you think the country's buses should run on Shabbat?

**Mosheh:** Absolutely not. When the buses don't run on Shabbat, you can feel the serenity. Our modern society should be guided by the ancient laws of our people.

**Sarah:** But we live in the modern world! Judaism is important, but our society should be governed by today's values. Without buses, I can't get around.

**Ya'akov:** Sarah: What do you think about how people dress in Israel?

**Sarah:** Everyone should dress however they like. It's often hot here, so I dress for comfort. Plus I like to find trendy clothes that match my style.

**Mosheh:** I appreciate that we live in a country where I can freely dress in religious clothing, like a long black coat and hat. I also believe in the value of modest dress—no matter how hot it is. It makes me feel uncomfortable when I encounter people dressed immodestly, showing too much bare skin.

**Ya'akov:** What are your thoughts about serving in the Israeli army?

**Mosheh:** Many in my community don't serve in the army. Instead, they study Torah. Studying Torah is the best way to serve and contribute to our nation's identity and well-being.

**Sarah:** I'm proud to have served in the army. I learned a great deal during my time as a soldier. Sadly, I know many people who have lost friends or family during their service. I think everyone should serve in the army—why should only some people have that burden and not others?

**Ya'akov:** Well, that's all the time we have. Thanks for listening to *Tough Questions with Ya'akov*!

## DISCUSS THE FOLLOWING QUESTIONS:

1. How would you answer each of Ya'akov's questions? How are your answers similar to or different than those of Mosheh and Sarah?

2. What do their answers tell you about life in Israel?

3. What other questions would you want to ask Mosheh and Sarah? How do you think they would answer?

# What Happens When Values Conflict?

Once a month, a group called Women of the Wall gather at the Kotel. A group of women coming together to pray is a sight that wouldn't raise eyebrows in most synagogues in America. But at the Kotel, it's complicated.

Women of the Wall (or WOW, for short) often get strong reactions. Other worshippers at the Kotel have shouted at them and thrown things at them to try to stop them from praying. The women have sometimes even been arrested.

The Kotel is run according to ultra-Orthodox Jewish laws. Those laws require men and women to pray separately. Women are not permitted to read Torah or wear a tallit.

The ultra-Orthodox explain that for thousands of years Jewish tradition has assigned different roles to men and women. Indeed, if women and men were mixed together at the Kotel, then, according to their traditions, the ultra-Orthodox wouldn't be able to pray there.

At the Kotel, women are not permitted to hold or read from a Torah scroll, and if a woman tries to wear a tallit, she is asked to remove it.

Rabbi Shmuel Rabinowitz, the rabbi in charge of the Kotel, explains, "The Western Wall is the only place shared by all Jewish people—and it is not the place to force or express a world view." He wishes that the Women of the Wall would "leave the disputes outside the plaza [of the Kotel] and let the people of Israel have one place where there are no protests...."

But other Jews point out that these restrictions run counter to the value of freedom of expression and deny women equal access. They believe protest is exactly what's called for.

Micha Eshet, one of the paratroopers who liberated the Kotel in the 1967 Six-Day War, is one of those protesters. "We liberated the wall for both men and women," Eshet says. "We can't stand by any longer when...Women of the Wall are forbidden to pray...."

Some Israelis have worked to find a compromise. A small section of the wall known as Robinson's Arch was set aside for mixed-gender prayer, where women could read from the Torah. But WOW objected that Robinson's Arch was not equivalent to the Kotel. It felt like a consolation prize.

So every month, the Women of the Wall continue to pray and protest, while others pray and protest back.

# Don't Debate; Negotiate!

Pair up with a friend and negotiate how to work out this issue. Have one person represent the concerns of each side: the ultra-Orthodox and Women of the Wall. Your challenge is to negotiate an agreement that best satisfies the competing needs of both parties.

List the main concerns of each party in the spaces below:

| Concerns of the ultra-Orthodox | Concerns of Women of the Wall |
| --- | --- |
|  |  |

After negotiation, what was the agreement that you came to?

_____

_____

In what way did it satisfy each party?

_____

_____

In what way did it disappoint each party?

_____

_____

## Talk about It!

1. How does having a government and society with so many differing opinions make Israel a stronger nation? A weaker one?

2. How would you feel about the religious laws if you lived in Israel? How do you think the laws might affect your life?

3. How might Israel be different if it didn't have democratic values? If it didn't have Jewish values?

**Chapter 5**

# It Was Built With Hope

*Rehovot, Israel, 2012*

Today, Israel is a vibrant and modern country that's home to the largest Jewish community in the world. But it wasn't always like that. For many years, Israel was full of swamps and rocky, sandy areas. And while there have always been Jews living in Israel, in 1920 just 5 percent of the population was Jewish.

## What Do You See?

With a partner, look at the two pictures of Rehovot and discuss:

1. How would you describe each one?

2. What do you think it would have been like to live in Rehovot in 1893? How about today?

*Rehovot, Israel, 1893*

# The Hope for a Home

Have you ever felt different from the rest of the crowd? Before 1948, many Jews around the world felt that way. Wherever they lived, they were a minority. And although they flourished in many places, in others they often suffered from anti-Semitism and discrimination. Many Jews dreamed of having a land of their own.

## First Aliyah

Some Jews decided to make their dream a reality, and between 1882 and 1903, many Jews moved to Eretz Yisrael, the Land of Israel, which was then part of the Ottoman Empire. Most came from eastern Europe, to escape violent anti-Semitism there. Others came from Yemen. This period of immigration was called the First Aliyah.

## By the Numbers:

In 1918, the total population of what is now Israel was 660,000 people. Today, 8.5 million people live there.

*Kibbutz Givat Brenner, 1936*

**1517–1917**
Ottoman Empire rules Palestine

**1882**
First Aliyah begins

**1895**
The Dreyfus Affair

**1897**
First Zionist Conference

**1904**
Second Aliyah begins

**1914–1918**
World War I

**1917**
Balfour Declaration

**1918–1948**
Britain rules Palestine

**1939**
The White Paper

**1939–1945**
World War II

**1948**
Establishment of modern State of Israel

*Delegates from seventeen countries at the First Zionist Congress*

*Alfred Dreyfus being stripped of his rank in a painting by Henri Meyer, 1895*

# Zionism

At the same time that the First Aliyah was taking place, Captain Alfred Dreyfus, a Jewish French soldier, was arrested in France for spying. Known as the Dreyfus Affair, his trial was widely criticized for its anti-Semitic bias. Although Captain Dreyfus was innocent, he was found guilty. Covering the trial, a young Jewish journalist named Theodor Herzl witnessed mobs outside the courthouse shouting, "Death to the Jews." Herzl came away from the experience profoundly affected.

## Building a Movement

The trial led Herzl to believe that Jews would only be safe if they had their own land, and he began to work hard to make that happen. In 1897, he organized the First Zionist Congress in Basel, Switzerland, to discuss strategies. A new movement was born—Zionism. Its goal was to create a homeland for the Jewish people.

*Theodor Herzl at the conference*

*"If you will it, it is no dream."*—**Theodor Herzl**

## Illustrate the Dream

Imagine that you are one of the original pioneers who came to the Land of Israel.

In the space above, draw a simple outline of a house. Inside the house, draw words, symbols, and colors that represent your new home in Israel. What will your new home provide for you that you didn't have in your old country?

## Taking Action

With Herzl as their leader, Zionists around the world worked to achieve their dream. They raised money for new communities in Palestine. They met with leaders around the world, asking them for their support. They even designed Israel's flag and wrote its national anthem, "Hatikvah" (The Hope). They had hope that their dream would become a reality.

*To raise money for a new Jewish homeland, tzedakah boxes, like this one from 1934, were distributed to Jewish homes around the world. By Word War II, there were over one million boxes in circulation.*

*The first kibbutz, Degania, 1910*

# Second Aliyah

Between 1904 and 1914, anti-Semitism in Russia and eastern Europe grew, leading to another, even larger, wave of Jews moving to Israel. This was called the Second Aliyah. Unlike the pioneers of the First Aliyah, who often employed local Arabs to work their farms, the immigrants of the Second Aliyah believed that to create a successful Jewish state, they needed to prove that they could make a home for themselves and not depend on others.

It wasn't easy. Many of the new immigrants had never been farmers before. The land was not ideal for farming. Illnesses such as cholera and malaria were common.

## The Kibbutz

Despite the challenges, these early pioneers had many successes. They built the city of Tel Aviv, printed newspapers, and opened schools. They also founded the first kibbutz, a cooperative community in which members worked and ate together, and even shared childcare, as if they were part of one large family.

*"We lead a curious life here. I do the same work every day. It is very boring. In the morning, as soon as I get up, I must stoke the stove, then boil the milk, peel the potatoes for the stew and cook some soup....Then I must do the dishes and sweep the room...I am often ill with malaria..."*

—**Anya**, an immigrant to Palestine, writing in her diary, December 1912

## Hebrew

The immigrants of the Second Aliyah made Hebrew the language of the land. Previously, Hebrew had mostly been the language of prayer and study. With immigrants coming from many different countries and speaking many different languages, Hebrew was a language they could all share.

*Eliezer Ben-Yehuda (1858–1922) led the movement to revive Hebrew as a language for everyday speech and even invented new, modern Hebrew words such as glidah for ice cream.*

## Moving Forward

Stand in a line with your friends. The object of the game is to get to the other side of the room. Imagine that you are all new immigrants to Israel in the early 1900s. On each turn, a player can ask a question such as, "How do I learn Hebrew?" or, "How will I make new friends?" Or, a player can choose to name one of the obstacles that the early pioneers faced, such as "hard labor" or "sickness." For every question a player asks, he or she takes three steps forward; for every obstacle named, all the other players must move back a step.

Once everyone has crossed the room, discuss:

1. How easy or hard was it to come up with questions? With obstacles?

2. How do you think the pioneers felt when faced with obstacles?

3. How do you think those early pioneers would feel if they could see the country of Israel today?

# The Arab Resistance

The Jewish community continued to purchase land and settle it, and its population steadily grew. In response, many Arabs became fearful that their country would be taken over by Jews and began refusing to do business with Jewish pioneers. Some Arabs even attacked Jewish communities, burning crops and killing people. To defend themselves, the Jewish community formed the Haganah, the first nationwide Jewish defense organization. It ultimately became the Israel Defense Forces, or IDF—Israel's army.

*Haganah fighters, 1948*

55

# Mixed Messages

After World War I, Palestine came under British rule, and the British were faced with the challenge of governing a population of both Arabs and Jews. The British sent inconsistent messages to both sides. Sometimes the British would tell one group one thing and the other group another. This led to much confusion.

### THE MCMAHON-HUSSEIN CORRESPONDENCE

In 1915, before Britain was even in control of the land, Sir Henry McMahon pledged to Hussein ibn Ali, the sharif of Mecca, that Britain would support Arab independence in "the land." While it was unclear which land his letters referred to, the Arabs believed it meant Israel.

### THE BALFOUR DECLARATION

In 1917, the British government committed to support a Jewish homeland in Palestine. Known as the Balfour Declaration, it gave hope to Zionists that their dream for a homeland would come to be.

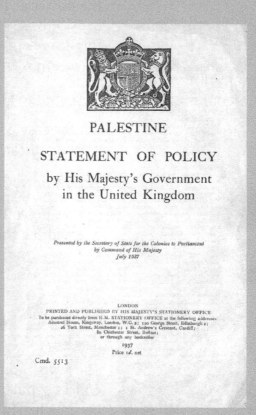

### THE WHITE PAPER

In 1939, Britain issued a declaration called the White Paper, which said that Palestine would be a single state with an Arab majority. To make sure that Arabs would remain the majority, the White Paper severely restricted Jewish immigration and the sale of land to Jews. It seemed to suggest that Arabs would always rule the land and led many Zionists to feel betrayed by the British.

*Jews arriving at the Auschwitz death camp in Poland, 1944*

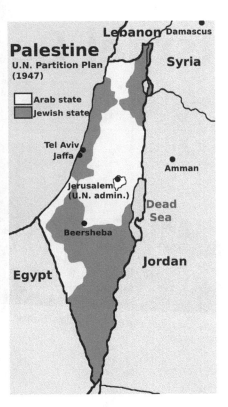

# After World War II

The White Paper could not have come at a worse time for the Jewish community. In 1939, as World War II was about to begin, and with Palestine's doors closed, the Jews of Europe had nowhere to escape. Six million Jews were murdered in the Holocaust, and hundreds of thousands of survivors became refugees with nowhere to go.

## Refugees

After the Holocaust, many survivors tried to return to their homes in Europe, but they weren't welcome. At the same time, the British continued to enforce their White Paper and stopped ships of Jewish refugees trying to get into Palestine.

*Full of Holocaust survivors headed to Palestine, the ship Exodus 1947 was stopped by the British. The sight of Holocaust survivors being forced to return to Germany helped turn world support in favor of a Jewish state.*

## The Partition Plan

Britain chose to turn its Palestine problem over to the United Nations, which recommended dividing Palestine into two separate states: one Arab, one Jewish. Jerusalem would not be a part of either state. Most Jewish leaders accepted the plan, happy at the prospect of having a Jewish state. But most Arab leaders rejected it and threatened to go to war if it was accepted. Since there were twice as many Arabs as Jews living in the land at the time, they felt that they should be given more land than they were offered. Despite the threats of war, the UN General Assembly voted in favor of the Partition Plan in 1947.

# Israel Becomes a State

*David Ben-Gurion reads the Israeli Declaration of Independence, 1948*

Not long after the United Nations voted "yes" for the Partition Plan, on the morning of May 14, 1948, Jews around the world gathered around radios to hear David Ben-Gurion, Israel's first prime minister, read the Israeli Declaration of Independence before a crowd in Tel Aviv. With tears in their eyes, the crowd sang the new nation's national anthem: "Hatikvah."

The Jewish state was no longer just a hope and a dream. It was the State of Israel.

## Hatikvah: The Hope

*As long as in the heart within,*

*A Jewish soul still yearns*

*And onward, toward the ends of the east*

*An eye still yearns toward Zion*

*Our hope is not yet lost*

*The hope of two thousand years*

*To be a free people in our land*

*The land of Zion and Jerusalem*

Watch a video of Hatikvah at bhlink.me/israel5

## Today's Hatikvah

The words of "Hatikvah" express the hopes of the early pioneers for a new Jewish state.

Imagine that it was your job to create a new anthem. Write it in the space above, as a poem or song. Then, using the "Hatikvah" melody, chant or sing your new anthem to your friends.

*Israel's Declaration of Independence*

# War of Independence

There was little time to celebrate. The new nation of Israel was attacked by five Arab countries—Egypt, Syria, Transjordan (now called Jordan), Lebanon, and Iraq.

Israel's soldiers successfully beat back the attack, and when the fighting ended, the Jewish homeland was here to stay.

**ISRAEL**
**WAR OF INDEPENDENCE**
Arab Attacks, 15 May - 10 June, 1948

*The red arrows show where the surrounding countries attacked Israel.*

*Approximately 750,000 Palestinian Arabs left their homes and became refugees. Some left out of fear; others because they were forced to. Still others because they thought they would have better lives in a different country.*

## By the Numbers:

During Israel's first three years of existence, almost 700,000 Jewish immigrants moved there. Half were Holocaust survivors from Europe. The other half were Jews from Arab countries, who often chose to come in response to the violence that was rising against Jews in the Muslim world.

# Independence Day: Celebrations?

*"These days are filled with symbols that have very different meanings for the two groups: victor and the vanquished, the Jews who won the war and the Arabs who lost the war."*

—**Nadia Kinani**, an Arab Israeli educator

**M**ay 14, 1948, was one of most joyous days in Jewish history. After two thousand years without a homeland, and after the horrors of the Holocaust, the Jewish people had their own country.

Today, Israelis and Jews worldwide celebrate Yom Ha'atzma'ut, Israeli Independence Day, with fireworks, street parties, and picnics.

*A child commemorating Nakba Day in Hebron*

In contrast, Palestinians call May 15, the day after Yom Ha'atzma'ut, the Nakba, which means "catastrophe." During the War of Independence, 750,000 Palestinians fled or were forced from their homes, and a Palestinian state was not created as the United Nations had intended.

Palestinians consider the Nakba a day of sorrow. Many commemorate it with rallies and speeches. Protesters carry cutouts of keys, symbolizing the keys to the homes Palestinians abandoned in 1948. Sometimes the rallies turn violent, with protestors burning tires, throwing rocks, and clashing with Israeli police.

In Israel, these two complicated realities—Yom Ha'atzma'ut and Nakba Day—exist side by side. Some celebrate Yom Ha'atzma'ut, and others commemorate the Nakba. "The celebration of the Jewish people's ability to govern itself without having to play the loyal minority is a legitimate celebration. At the same time, it is worth recognizing the political challenges and the human cost that statehood created," says writer and activist Ariel Beery.

*Americans celebrating Yom Ha'atzma'ut*

# May 14, 1948

# May 15, 1948

## Dear Diary

With a partner, imagine that one of you is an Israeli Jew and the other a Palestinian Arab. Above are two days of your diary, May 14 (the date of the Israeli Declaration of Independence) and May 15 (when war broke out). On each page, answer the following questions:

- How are you feeling on this day?

- What events have you witnessed?

- What are your friends or family members saying?

- What are you hearing and reading in the news?

Then, trade diary entries with your partner and discuss:

- What was similar about your entries?

- What was different?

## Talk about It!

1. What do you think the pioneers from over one hundred years ago would think if they saw Israel today? How might they feel?

2. Why do you think many Jewish people who live outside of Israel celebrate Yom Ha'atzma'ut?

3. What ritual would you create that Jews could do on Yom Ha'atzma'ut to recognize the Nakba while still celebrating Israel's independence?

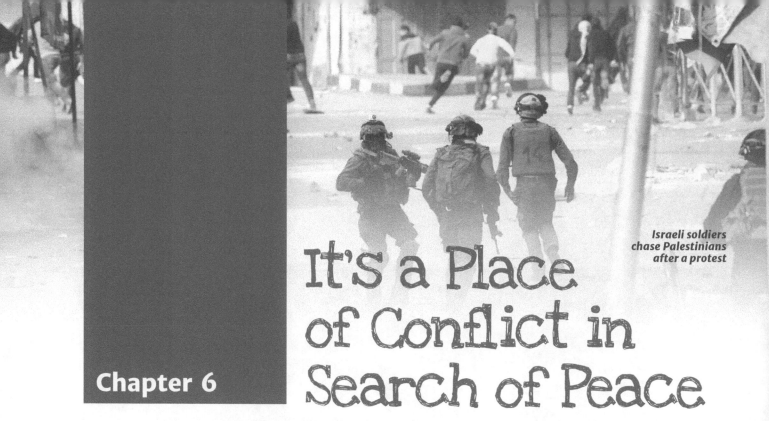

*Israeli soldiers chase Palestinians after a protest*

# It's a Place of Conflict in Search of Peace

**Chapter 6**

Imagine that you live in a neighborhood where no one wants to be your friend; in fact, everyone really wants you to leave. That's how Israelis sometimes feel. Many of their neighbors—Iraq, Syria, Lebanon, Jordan, and Egypt—have fought wars against Israel. The Palestinians in the West Bank and Gaza have protested against Israel, sometimes peacefully, sometimes violently.

*Palestinian and Jewish students from the Music In Common program*

## What Do You See?

With a partner, discuss the two photos on this page:

1. How do these photos make you feel?

2. What conclusions might you come to about the Israeli-Palestinian relationship based only on the first photo? On the second photo?

3. Using both photos as your information source, how would you describe the relationship between Jews and Palestinians in Israel?

# Israel Defense Forces

In Israel, most men and women are required to join the Israel Defense Forces (IDF) at age eighteen. Rich or poor, recent immigrant or longtime resident, Jewish and Druze, Israelis from all walks of life serve their country together. Arab Israelis who wish to volunteer also serve. For Arab Israelis and religious Jews, there is also an option of participating in Israel's national service program and assisting at places like schools, hospitals, or nursing homes.

*IDF soldiers at their swearing-in ceremony at the Western Wall*

## After High School

What are some of the things you'd like to do after you graduate high school? On a separate piece of paper, draw a line down the middle to create two sections. In the first section, use pictures, colors, and words to express your feelings about the possibilities.

Now imagine you live in Israel and you will be joining the army after high school. In the second section, create a new image to express how you would feel. What would excite you? What concerns might you have about joining?

## The Challenges

The IDF has achieved great victories and maintained the security of Israel and its people. It has responded to every type of attack imaginable: stabbings, stonings, bus bombings, drone attacks, chemical threats, rocket attacks, invading armies, and more. Amidst these conflicts, the IDF strives to balance Israel's security needs with its humanitarian duty to protect civilians on all sides.

## Text Study: The Values of the IDF

Read the text below with a friend and discuss the questions:

*"The IDF...will act in a judicious and safe manner... out of recognition of the supreme value of human life....IDF soldiers will not use their weapons and force to harm human beings who are not combatants or prisoners of war, and will do all in their power to avoid causing harm to [them]...."*

—from the **IDF's Code of Ethics and Mission**

1. The IDF's job is to keep Israel's citizens safe. Do you think the IDF's code of ethics makes that job easier or harder? Why?

2. Judaism teaches that *piku'ach nefesh*, the saving of a life, takes precedence over almost anything else. How do you see this value reflected in the text?

# Conflict and Peace: A Visual Timeline

Over the years, many have tried to make peace and solve conflicts in the Middle East. But disagreement and distrust remain. Peace has not yet come to the region.

## 1948–9 WAR OF INDEPENDENCE

Israel prevails. Fighting ends without a formal peace treaty.

## 1956 SUEZ WAR

*IDF soldiers, 1956*

## 1964 PALESTINE LIBERATION ORGANIZATION FORMS

Palestinians create the Palestine Liberation Organization, or PLO, to represent them. Their original goals include the destruction of Israel.

## 1967 SIX–DAY WAR

In response to serious threats, Israel attacks Egypt, Jordan, and Syria, and defeats their armies in just six days. Israel gains new territories, including the Gaza Strip, the West Bank, and East Jerusalem. Israel offers to return territory in exchange for peace, but the Arab nations refuse.

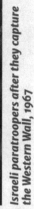

*Israeli paratroopers after they capture the Western Wall, 1967*

## 1973 YOM KIPPUR WAR

Egypt and Syria launch a surprise attack. Israel suffers high casualties but ultimately wins the war and keeps the territory it captured in 1967.

*Egyptian soldiers, 1973*

## 1979 ISRAEL–EGYPT PEACE TREATY

Israel agrees to return the Sinai Peninsula to Egypt in exchange for peace.

*President Sadat and Prime Minister Begin, 1979*

## 1981 EGYPTIAN PRESIDENT ANWAR SADAT IS ASSASSINATED

## 1982 FIRST LEBANON WAR

The PLO attacks Israel from its base in Lebanon. Israel responds by invading Lebanon. It maintains a presence there for eighteen years.

## 1987 FIRST INTIFADA

Palestinians protest and riot in response to the Israeli presence on the West Bank and in Gaza.

## 1987 HAMAS FORMS

A new organization, Hamas, is formed to represent Palestinians. Hamas gains support because they operate schools and hospitals, and provide other services that help with everyday life for Palestinians. However, their attacks on civilians and calls for the destruction of Israel lead the United States and many other countries to consider them a terrorist organization.

## 1991 MADRID PEACE CONFERENCE

The United States and Soviet Union organize a peace conference with Israel and its Arab neighbors. For the first time, negotiators from Israel and the Palestinians meet with one another. The idea

*President H.W. Bush addessing the conference, 1991*

of a two-state solution—one Israeli and one Palestinian—is discussed.

## 1994 ISRAEL–JORDAN PEACE TREATY SIGNED

*Israeli Prime Minister Yitzhak Rabin and King Hussein of Jordan, with US President Bill Clinton, 1994*

## 1995 YITZHAK RABIN, PRIME MINISTER OF ISRAEL, IS ASSASSINATED

## 1996 PALESTINIAN ELECTIONS

Palestinians conduct fair and free elections. Israel withdraws from parts of the West Bank.

## 2000 CAMP DAVID SUMMIT

*Prime Minister Ehud Barak of Israel, US President Bill Clinton, and Chairman Yasser Arafat at Camp David, 2000*

Yasser Arafat, the leader of the PLO, meets with Israeli Prime Minister Ehud Barak at Camp David, in Maryland. Their peace talks break down over the issues of control of Jerusalem and whether Palestinians should be given land inside Israel.

## 1993 OSLO ACCORDS

The PLO rejects terrorism and, for the first time, recognizes Israel's right to exist. Israel agrees to allow the PLO's newly formed Palestinian Authority to rule the Gaza Strip and parts of the West Bank.

*Israeli Prime Minister Yitzhak Rabin and PLO Chairman Yasser Arafat, with US President Bill Clinton, 1993*

## 2000 ISRAEL WITHDRAWS FROM LEBANON

## 2000 SECOND INTIFADA

In response to the failure of the peace talks, Palestinians begin the Second Intifada, which includes suicide bombings against Israeli civilians.

*The aftermath of a suicide bombing attack on an Israeli bus, 2000*

*The security fence*

## 2002 ISRAEL BUILDS A SECURITY FENCE

Israel begins building a fence to prevent terrorists from entering the country. The barrier does its job but provokes controversy because it is built, in part, on land claimed by Palestinians and makes daily life more difficult for Palestinians.

## 2005 ISRAEL WITHDRAWS FROM GAZA

Israel dismantles settlements in Gaza and withdraws its soldiers, leaving the Palestinian Authority in charge.

*Israeli residents of Gaza protesting the IDF's withdrawal, 2005*

## 2006 SECOND LEBANON WAR

*"The hundreds of Israeli military closures across the West Bank such as checkpoints, road-blocks, and settler-only roads...make simple daily tasks for Palestinians who are trying to get to work, school or hospital a constant struggle."*
**—Amnesty International**

## 2007 HAMAS TAKE-OVER OF GAZA

Hamas violently overthrows the Palestinian Authority in Gaza. Palestinian rule is divided, with the Palestinian Authority in charge of the West Bank and Hamas in charge of Gaza. Hamas fires rockets into Israel from Gaza, hitting nearby towns.

*"One of the biggest problems that ALL Palestinians complain about is the lack of a clear future.... [W]e have lived through periods of hope, violence, anticipation, concern...We do not know what the future holds for us...."*
**—Nedal Zahran**, a Palestinian from the West Bank

## 2008 OPERATION CAST LEAD

Israeli soldiers enter Gaza and destroy Hamas rockets.

*Remains of some of the thousands of rockets fired on the Israeli city of Sderot from the Gaza Strip*

> "I remember growing up, feeling safe and secure in Sderot. I was happy. Why can't my kids have that kind of childhood?"
>
> —**Carmit Malka,** an Israeli from Sderot

## 2014 OPERATION PROTECTIVE EDGE

Following the murder of three Israeli teenagers by Hamas, Israel enters Gaza and destroys dozens of tunnels leading from Gaza into Israeli neighborhoods.

*Eyal Yifrah (19), Gilad Shaer (16), and Naftali Frenkel (16)*

## 2018 GAZA BORDER PROTESTS

Palestinians organize what they call the "Great March of Return," protests demanding that Palestinian refugees and their descendants be allowed to claim land in Israel.

# The Timeline

Continue the timeline into the future.

What do you think will happen between Israel and its neighbors in the future? In the white boxes, write the year and the title of an important event that you think will occur in five years, ten years, and twenty-five years. Add a drawing or paste an image that illustrates it.

IN FIVE YEARS, THE YEAR WILL BE: _____

THE EVENT: _____

IN TWENTY-FIVE YEARS, THE YEAR WILL BE: _____

THE EVENT: _____

IN TEN YEARS, THE YEAR WILL BE: _____

THE EVENT: _____

# Do Settlements Promote Security or Conflict?

**What are the Settlements?** When Israel first captured the West Bank, many Israeli leaders hoped that they would be able to return it in exchange for peace. Others believed that the West Bank was a part of ancient Israel and argued that the country should keep and settle it.

As time passed, the Israeli government encouraged citizens to move to the West Bank and build communities there, called settlements. Some Israeli Jews moved for religious reasons, while others moved because it was an affordable place to live or because it was close to their workplaces.

Today, there are more than 130 settlements. They range in size from tiny outposts to large cities. Many settlements are very close to major Israeli centers, while others are more remote.

> "I think the settlements are part of Israel....and I think the settlers view themselves as Israelis, and Israel views the settlers as Israelis."
>
> —**David Friedman**,
> US ambassador to Israel

**Are the Settlements an Obstacle to Peace?** Over the past decades, one of the most common suggestions for solving the Israeli-Palestinian conflict has been what is sometimes called the "two-state solution," or "two states for two peoples." This solution calls for the West Bank and Gaza to separate from Israel and become an independent country, called Palestine.

The settlements cause many to question whether Israel is really open to the two-state solution. After all, they argue, if the West Bank someday becomes a part of a Palestinian state, then the Jewish homes and communities in those settlements would need to be dismantled.

**Are the Settlements Necessary for Israel's Security?** Many Israelis fear what would happen if the settlements were dismantled. When Israel dismantled its settlements in Gaza in 2005, many hoped that would be a first step toward peace. But instead, the opposite occurred. Gaza became a base for Hamas, which uses the territory to launch missile attacks against Israel.

Israel argues that keeping the settlements in the West Bank is necessary to provide security for Israel's citizens. Much of Israel's population can be reached by a missile launched from the West Bank, and Israel can't risk letting this land fall under the control of Hamas or another group that seeks to destroy Israel.

*The Ma'ale Adumim, settlement and the Arab village Al-Eizariya*

> *"Nearly 90,000 settlers are living... in the middle of what, by any reasonable definition, would be the future Palestinian state."*

—**John Kerry**,
former US secretary of state

# Debate It!

Your friend Adi's family is planning to move to Israel. Her father wants to live in the West Bank because it's more affordable. Her mother thinks Jewish people shouldn't live in the West Bank because it makes the peace process more challenging. Adi doesn't know what to think.

Should Adi's family move to the settlements?

With a partner, debate the issue. List the main points in the spaces below.

**YES:** Adi's family should move to the West Bank:

_____

_____

**NO:** Adi's family should move elsewhere in Israel:

_____

_____

## Talk about It!

There's a famous story in the Talmud about Rabbi Hillel. A man who wanted to convert to Judaism asked Rabbi Hillel to explain the whole Torah while the man stood on one foot. Hillel responded: "What is hateful to you, do not do to your neighbor. The rest is commentary. Now, go study."

Use this story to answer the following questions:

1. Imagine someone asked you to explain the conflicts described in this chapter while standing on one foot—in other words, to sum them up very briefly. What would you say?

2. How do you think the people who live in the Middle East might benefit from Rabbi Hillel's advice?

# It's a Part of the World Community

# Chapter 7

Is there a food that you think is delicious, but when your friends taste it they make a face? For people and even governments around the world, Israel inspires very different reactions. Some people think of Israel and smile. Some get angry. Others switch back and forth. Even though it's a small country, people across the globe have strong opinions about Israel and its people.

## What Do You See?

Around the world, some people celebrate Israel while others protest it. With a partner, look at the pictures and discuss:

1. How does it feel to see that some of the people protesting are Jewish?

2. If you could speak with one of the protestors or with one of Israel's supporters, what would you want to ask? What would you want to say?

3. These kinds of images are shared in the media around the world. How do you think seeing them affects people's opinions of Israel?

Angola's embassy in Tel Aviv, Israel

Israel's embassy in Washington, DC

# On the World Stage

Israelis have relationships with people around the world. They buy and sell one another's products, collaborate on scientific projects, and study and teach in each other's universities. Comedians and musicians from around the world often perform in Israel, and Israeli artists tour the globe.

Israel also has political ties with other countries. When a relationship between countries is positive and healthy, they will send representatives, called ambassadors, to each other's countries.

Cornell Tech's campus in New York City

*" Thanks to this outstanding partnership and ground-breaking proposal from Cornell and the Technion [in Israel], New York City's goal of becoming the global leader in technological innovation is now within sight."*

—**Michael Bloomberg**, former mayor of New York City

## Video Review

When comedian Conan O'Brien visited Israel, he created videos aboout his trip. Visit bhlink.me/israel7 to see them. Pick one and write a review of it in the space below.

☆ ☆ ☆ ☆ ☆

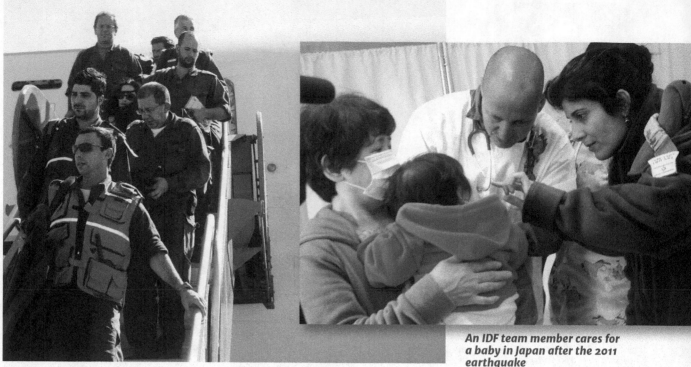

*IDF Medical Corps arriving in Haiti after the 2010 earthquake*

*An IDF team member cares for a baby in Japan after the 2011 earthquake*

# Lifesaving around the World

When there is a disaster someplace in the world, like an earthquake, flood, or terrorist attack, Israel is often among the first countries to send help. Over the years, Israelis have helped save thousands of lives in countries such as Haiti, Nepal, Japan, and the United States.

Israeli volunteers have even chosen to bring help to people in countries that consider Israel an enemy, like Syria. The Israeli organization Israel Flying Aid has given millions of dollars of medical supplies, tents, baby formula, and clothing to victims of the Syrian civil war.

## Values in Action

Watch the video at bhlink.me/israel7 about the work of Israeli organizations, such as the IDF Medical Corps, around the world.

1. What values do you think inspire Israelis to do this work and the work shown in the photos above?

2. In what ways do you think these experiences affect relationships between Israelis and people around the world?

3. In what ways did watching the video and seeing these photos affect your own feelings about Israel?

## Negative Opinions around the World

Despite Israel's positive relationships with many countries around the world, some people are still distrustful and even hostile to Israel. Some feel that way because they strongly disagree with Israeli government policies. Other times, people's thoughts about Israel, the only Jewish country in the world, are influenced by anti-Semitism.

These negative feelings have even flared up at the United Nations, which declared in 1975 that Zionism was racism. It revoked that statement in 1991. However, it continues to single out Israel and has voted to condemn Israel more times than any other country, including terrible regimes, like North Korea, that have hurt and imprisoned many of their citizens.

*"Supporters of Israel feel that it is harshly judged, by standards that are not applied to its enemies—and too often this is true, particularly in some UN bodies."*

—**Kofi Anan**, former secretary-general of the United Nations

### Headlines and Israel

Find a recent Twitter post, blog post, or news article that criticizes Israel. Discuss with a partner:

1. How does it feel to see Israel criticized in the news?

2. What criticisms does the tweet or article make against Israel?

3. Do you think the criticism is fair or unfair? Why?

4. Now, find a second article, from a different news source, that reports a story from a perspective that is favorable to Israel.

5. Do you think the positive descriptions in the article are fair or unfair? Why?

*"...In an enemy country like Syria we have a full undercover unit, all native Arabic speakers— these people are fully committed to saving lives, as reflected in the Jewish culture and religion."*

—**Gal Lusky**, founder and CEO, Israel Flying Aid

# Protesting and Supporting

Israel is a country that people have strong feelings about. People on all sides of the many issues affecting Israel sign petitions, attend rallies and protests, and write letters to their representatives in government.

*"Join with me... to declare a cultural boycott on Israel... to support all our brothers and sisters in Palestine and Israel who are struggling to end all forms of Israeli oppression."*

—**Roger Waters** of the band Pink Floyd

## In Critique

Some groups try to convince the Israeli government to change its policies. For example, the organization J Street will sometimes ask politicians in America to turn down requests from the Israeli government. J Street's goals are to promote peace in the region and make Israel a better place, while supporting Israel's right to exist and defend itself from attacks.

## In Opposition

The BDS (Boycott, Divestment, Sanctions) movement, in contrast, is highly critical of Israel and its policies. It works to convince governments and individuals to stop cooperating with Israel in any way. Advocates of the BDS movement call for boycotting Israel (refusing to buy products made in Israel), divestment from Israel (stopping investment in Israeli companies), and sanctions against Israel (making laws to punish Israel).

For example, BDS advocates have worked to have Israeli products removed from store shelves, asked colleges around the world to ban Israeli speakers, and pressured musicians not to perform in Israel. BDS supporters say their goals are to pressure Israel to allow Palestinians to return to homes in Israel that they or their parents or grandparents left when Israel became a state. However, BDS advocates typically do not consider Israel's security needs or even recognize its right to exist.

The fact that some BDS groups have chosen to criticize Israel for violating human rights, and no other countries, has led many to reject them as unfair and even anti-Semitic.

*"Israelis will be right to ask why cultural boycotts are not also being proposed against—to take random examples—North Korea and Zimbabwe, whose leaders are not generally considered paragons by the international community."*

—**J. K. Rowling**, author of the Harry Potter series

## In Support

Many organizations support Israel. Some collect funds for charities in Israel, host Israel parades, and speak with politicians on Israel's behalf. Some arrange for Israeli speakers and teachers to visit American schools and form relationships between American students and Israelis.

There is also a movement called "Buy Israel," which works to counter the calls of BDS. "Buy Israel" encourages people to buy Israeli products as a way to support Israeli companies.

*"We do not support the boycott of Israel...We have relations with Israel, we have mutual recognition of Israel."*

—**Mahmoud Abbas**, president of the Palestinian Authority

## Opinions in the Family

Interview two adults in your family (perhaps a parent and a grandparent) about their relationship to Israel.

- How would they describe their relationship with the State of Israel? With its people?

- What's their favorite thing about Israel?

- What concerns do they have about Israel?

- Do they disagree with any of Israel's policies?

- How do they feel about criticizing Israel?

After you speak with family members, take videos of them on a smartphone. Ask them to summarize their ideas by answering the questions again, in less than one minute each.

Then, share the videos with a partner and discuss the following questions:

1. Were any of the answers surprising to you?

2. Which opinions matched your own views? Were there any with which you disagreed?

3. In what ways did the relatives agree with one another? Disagree?

4. How did hearing different opinions on the same topic impact your own views?

# Can We Criticize Israel?

Israel faces intense scrutiny from critics around the world. Sometimes, a double standard seems to apply, and criticism crosses into anti-Semitism. "Anti-Semitism is alive and well, and increasingly it masquerades as criticism of Israel," says Rabbi Jill Jacobs, executive director of the human rights organization T'ruah.

But even Israel's most ardent supporters do not agree with everything it does. Is it fair to criticize Israel when it already faces so much hostility? Does further criticism only hurt Israel in the end? Or, does criticism put pressure on Israel to live up to its own values? Deciding when and how to critique Israel is complicated.

Some Jews feel it is wrong to criticize Israel, arguing that it fuels anti-Israel sentiments. They say that since Jews make up such a small percentage of the world's population, like a family, they need to support one another at all times. Jennifer Laszlo Mizrahi, founder and president of the Israel Project, put it this way, "We need to have their backs."

But many other Jews believe that respectful criticism should be encouraged, as it shows care for the country, its people, and its future. "The worst thing I see in some American Jews is apathy to what's happening in the only sovereign Jewish state on the planet," says Anat Hoffman, Israeli activist.

Such critics draw a distinction between arguing against a particular Israeli policy and against the country of Israel as a whole. Most importantly, says writer Hillel Halkin, "When you criticize Israel, you have to be careful not to do it in terms that may be usurped by forces that hate not only Israel, but all Jews...."

# Debate It!

Imagine that you are writing an article about Israel for your school newspaper. Is it okay to criticize Israel in your article? Take one side, and have a partner take the other. Debate the issue. List the main points that you each made in the spaces below.

YES! I can criticize Israel because:

_____

_____

_____

NO! I shouldn't be critical of Israel because:

_____

_____

_____

Then, discuss a third possibility with your partner:

MAYBE! It's sometimes okay to criticize Israel, but not always. When do you think it would be okay? When would it not be okay?

_____

_____

_____

## Talk about It!

1. In what ways did your own opinions about Israel change after you heard the stories in this chapter?

2. If you were going to work to support Israel, how would you choose to do so?

3. If you were going to criticize Israel, how would you choose to do so?

*The Israeli company M-Systems invented the first flash drive in 1999.*

*Professors at Israel's Hebrew University developed today's tasty variety of the cherry tomato.*

# Chapter 8

# It's Creative and Innovative

Do you text? Store your files on a USB flash drive? Snack on cherry tomatoes? Have you ever played the game Guess Who? That probably seems like a pretty random set of questions, but all of those products have something in common: They were developed by Israelis.

## What Do You See?

All the photos on this page show products that were invented or developed by Israelis. With a friend, discuss:

1. Which of these is most exciting to you?

2. Which one do you think was the most innovative? Why?

*A projection keyboard; Rummikub; and Bamba, a peanuty snack*

# Building the Economy

In Israel's early days, the government owned almost everything—many businesses, banks, the telephone company, the electric company, even the country's single airline. Under that system, Israel's economy went through many ups and downs. Families sometimes had trouble making ends meet. Many people were poor and had to rely on charitable donations from Jewish communities around the world.

## Creating Opportunity

Israeli leaders wanted to strengthen the economy and provide better jobs and living conditions for all Israelis. They took many steps. Perhaps most importantly, they shifted the country closer to a capitalist system—the kind of economic system we're used to in the United States and Canada. Government-owned businesses were sold to individual people, or groups of people, who developed their own products and services, rather than just operating the way the government told them to.

## Encouraging Innovation

Israeli leaders also chose to give money to creative Israeli companies. If they could help those companies come up with new ideas, then those companies would be successful and grow. And, if the companies grew, then more people in Israel would have jobs, and families would have what they needed to thrive.

## Improvise and Innovate

Step 1: Set a timer for five minutes. In small groups, try to think of ideas for new inventions of any kind. Make a list of your group's ideas.

Step 2: Collect five random objects from around the room, like a backpack, cardboard box, or plastic fork. Put them in the middle of your group. Reset the timer for five minutes and try to come up with a list of ideas: new uses for these five objects. For example, you can use the fork to comb your hair, or you can use the box to carry a puppy. Write these ideas down on a second list.

Then discuss the following questions with your group:

1. Why is coming up with new ideas difficult? What makes it easier?

2. Did having the objects in front of you make it easier to innovate?

3. In what ways do you think having support from the government can help companies innovate?

# Israeli Innovations

Today Israel has one of the world's leading economies. Many of its citizens are prosperous, and Israelis have created new inventions and contributed to the world in many different areas.

## Medical Innovations

Israelis have made major innovations in medical technology that help people live healthier lives all over the world.

### DIAGNOSIS

The PillCam is a tiny camera that's so small patients can swallow it like a pill so that doctors can get a look at their insides. It was invented by the Israeli company Given Imaging.

### TREATMENT

Claire Lomas, who is a paraplegic, walked across the finish line of the London Marathon wearing her ReWalk, a robotic exoskeleton that was developed by the Israeli company Argo Medical Technologies.

# Environmental Innovations

Israeli scientists have also innovated products that help protect the environment.

## By the Numbers:

Today, drip technology is used in 112 countries around the world.

### SOLAR

Taking advantage of Israel's hot, sunny climate, Israeli scientists have pioneered technologies that use the sun as an energy source. For example, Israeli window company Pythagoras Solar helps generate energy by building solar panels right into their windows.

### WATER

When Israeli engineer Simcha Blass noticed a tree in the desert growing bigger than its neighbors, he wondered why. He soon discovered that it was fed by a leaking water pipe. That gave him the idea to invent drip irrigation, which allows farmers to deliver water directly to the roots of plants—just like that leaky pipe did.

### CONSERVATION

Israeli company SodaStream creates home appliances that allow people to turn tap water into carbonated drinks, instead of buying drinks in plastic bottles.

# High-Tech Innovations

### TRANSPORTATION

Waze, the first GPS system to use crowdsourcing to help drivers avoid traffic, was invented in Israel.

### ROBOTICS

Flytrex is an Israeli company that builds drones that can deliver small packages.

### COMMUNICATION

ICQ, one of the first inter-netwide instant messaging services, was developed by five young entrepreneurs in Israel.

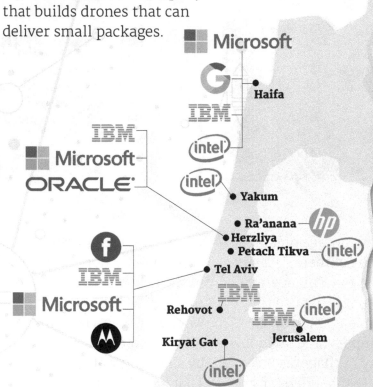

Microsoft

G • Haifa

IBM

(intel)

IBM

Microsoft

ORACLE

(intel) • Yakum

• Ra'anana hp

• Herzliya

• Petach Tikva (intel)

f

IBM • Tel Aviv

Microsoft

Rehovot • IBM IBM (intel)

Kiryat Gat • Jerusalem

(intel)

## By the Numbers:

Over three hundred global companies have offices in Israel.

*Netta Barzilai at the Eurovision song contest*

"*We don't have a lot of fabric options to buy [in Israel] so we use technology, digital printing, embroidery, knitting and beading to make materials of our own.*"

—**Corali Gat**, Israeli fashion designer

*Israeli fashion designer Corali Gat sewed hologram flowers into this garment.*

## Artistic Creativity

Israelis also contribute to fields like fashion, the arts, television, and web design. With the Israeli platform Wix, you can design your own website; you can easily fill up your Netflix queue with Israeli television shows like *Fauda*, *Srugim*, and more; Netta Barzilai, an Israeli musician, won the 2018 Eurovision contest with her innovative song "Toy" (hear it at bhlink.me/israel8); and fashion designers in Israel often make use of Israel's high-tech know-how to create unique fashion statements.

## Creative Crafting

Visit the crafting marketplace Etsy.com and find an Israeli crafter's shop (just type in "Israeli" or go to bhlink.me/israel8 for suggestions). Print out a photo of a product that you find appealing. Bring it in, and share it with a friend. Then, discuss:

1. Why did you pick the product you did?

2. What about the product is unique and innovative? Did its uniqueness contribute to why you found it appealing?

3. Does anything feel Israeli about the product you picked? What makes something "feel Israeli"?

4. Tape a picture of your product in the space below, and write a short description of it, explaining its appeal.

# Why Israel?

When a farmer plants seeds, crops can grow. The Israeli government planted the seeds for innovation and success in Israel by investing in Israeli companies. But to thrive, plants also need sun, water, and good soil. In Israel, the economy was able to grow because other factors in Israeli society helped make it possible. Here are some of them:

*Student researcher at the Weizmann Institute of Science*

## A Culture of Learning

Historically, the Jewish people have placed a high value on education, and it was no different for the founders of Israel. As they built the country, they also opened schools and universities. Israel has an educated population that is ready to learn, create, and innovate.

## A Community Network

Most people in Israel spend time in the army after high school. There they meet other Israelis from every walk of life. This gives them a network of friends that they can call on, even after they leave the army. So, if you are an Israeli starting up a new company and need advice from someone with a special skill, you can probably pick up the phone and find the help you need.

## Immigrants

Israel's culture of innovation has also benefited from the skills and knowledge that immigrants have brought into the country. For example, when thousands of Russians immigrated to Israel in the 1990s, they brought their skills as mathematicians, doctors, engineers, artists, and musicians with them and added to Israel's productivity.

*"Everybody knows everybody; everybody was serving in the army with the brother of everybody; the mother of everybody was the teacher in their school...."*

—**Yossi Vardi**, Israeli business leader, from *Start-up Nation*, a book by Dan Senor and Saul Singer

# It's Okay to Fail

In Israel, it's often considered acceptable to fail...as long as you learn from your mistakes and try again! Israeli business leader Menny Barzilay puts it this way: "We don't see failure as a big deal. If you fail three times...and you come to me and want me to invest in your fourth company, I'll probably consider you as someone with a lot of experience...compared with a kid who has never tried once."

## Failure As a Building Block

Divide into groups. Each group should have an equal number of wooden building blocks or other stackable item, such as paper cups. Then, start a three-minute timer and race to build the tallest tower possible.

Afterward, discuss with your group what worked well and what you could do better, documenting your answers below.

| What worked | What we should do next time |
|---|---|
|  |  |
|  |  |
|  |  |

Then, set the timer for another three minutes and build a new tower. The group that has the tallest standing tower at the end of this round wins.

Afterward, discuss:

1. In what ways did your experience in the first round make your towers more successful the second time?

2. Think about a time in your own life when you failed at something. What did you learn from the experience? In what ways did the failure help lead to other successes?

## By the numbers:

Israel has been ranked the second most educated country in the world. (Canada is ranked first.)

87

# Does Israel's Economy Help Everyone?

"Tech titan"

HELLO
my name is
"Small but mighty"

"Start-up nation"

These are some of Israel's nicknames, and for good reason. Israel has one of the world's strongest economies, with more newly established businesses, called start-ups, than any country in the world other than the United States.

Yet, while there are more millionaires in Israel than ever, one in five Israelis is considered poor, the highest percentage of any developed nation. "Israel...somehow manages to be a 'start-up nation,' with high economic growth; yet, at the same time, it remains a backward nation with many extremely poor families," says political commentator Shmuel Rosner.

The largest number of poor families can be found among two groups: 59 percent of ultra-Orthodox Jews and 58 percent of Arab Israelis live below the poverty line. In contrast, only about 5 percent of other Jewish Israelis are poor.

There are many complicated reasons for this inequity. For example, the ultra-Orthodox choose to send their children to schools that don't teach secular topics such as math and science, and therefore they are not prepared for high-tech jobs. Another factor is that, in general, neither the ultra-Orthodox nor Arab Israelis serve in the Israeli military, which leaves them out of community networks that others find very helpful. Also, families in both groups often choose to have many children that they then struggle to feed, clothe, and house.

Jewish tradition places a high priority on the value of

tzedakah. While many choose to translate *tzedakah* as "charity," the Hebrew word more closely translates to *tzedek*, "justice." Judaism teaches that it is just and a moral obligation to ensure that the poor are cared for. As one anti-poverty advocate, Gidi Kroch, says, "[Poverty] just does not fit with our Israeli culture and our Jewish identity. It is not our way."

# Debate It!

Israel has chosen to invest resources in technology and start-ups. Is that the best choice?

Take one side, and have a partner take the other. Debate the issue. In the spaces below, list the main points that you each made.

YES: Israel's choice to invest in technology has helped build a country where many are able to thrive and succeed.

_____

_____

NO: The government should be using its resources to help the needy, rather than its corporations.

_____

_____

After listening to all the arguments, did your own position change? Why or why not?

_____

_____

## Talk about It!

1. Pick three inventions from this chapter that were the most interesting to you. What was innovative and unique about each of them?

2. Compare what you know about Israel's culture of innovation to the culture of your own hometown or school. In what ways are they similar? Different?

3. What helps you be creative? What can you do to help others be their most creative?

| Chapter 9 | # It's a Place to See |
| --- | --- |

Think of the best vacation spot you've ever gone to. What made it wonderful? Whatever it was, Israel probably has some of that too. Beautiful beaches? Check. Great museums? Check. Hiking? Sports? World-class entertainment? Check, check, and check. Throw in some only-in-Israel uniqueness, and it's clear: Israel is a place to see.

# Who Comes?

For many Jews from around the world, visiting Israel is an important part of their Jewish life. Some come as part of a family vacation. Others choose to celebrate their bar or bat mitzvah in Israel. Still others visit with teen tour groups like the ones run by NFTY, USY, BBYO, and NCSY, among others. There are also special tours called Taglit–Birthright Israel, which provide a free trip to Israel for Jewish people between the ages of eighteen and twenty-six.

Many non-Jews also visit Israel. Some come to see sites that are holy to their own religions. Some come to visit the museums and see the archaeological sites. Some just come to have fun.

# מספרים

## By the Numbers:

Each year, over 3.5 million visitors come to Israel.

# Design a Tour

Imagine you are a tour leader, hired to create a one-week itinerary, or plan, for customers going to Israel. You need to design the perfect trip that will help your customers experience Israel and develop an emotional connection with it.

Step 1: Complete the charts below.

| My customer is (circle all that apply): | | |
|---|---|---|
| Jewish | Christian | Muslim |
| religious | North American | a family with children |
| a group of college kids | a young couple | other |

| My theme for this itinerary (circle all that apply): | | |
|---|---|---|
| modern | ancient | fun |
| nature | Jewish | other |

Step 2: Do your research. On the following pages are images of some of the most popular sites in Israel. Scan the QR codes to visit the website for each one and complete the questions. You can also find more great sites to explore and add to your tour at bhlink.me/israel9.

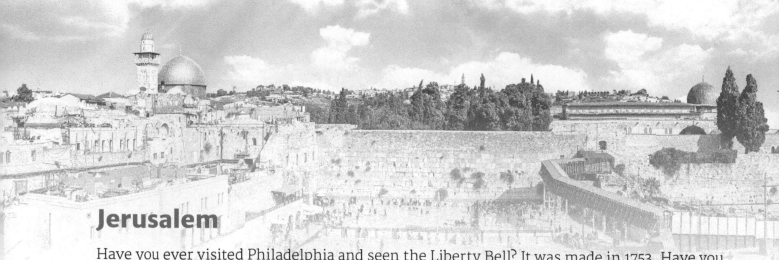

# Jerusalem

Have you ever visited Philadelphia and seen the Liberty Bell? It was made in 1753. Have you visited the White House in Washington, DC? The cornerstone was laid in 1792. In the US, those are considered very old, historic attractions. But in Jerusalem, there are buildings, archaeological sites, and artifacts that are thousands of years old. It's a city with both ancient and modern sites. Here are just some of them:

**SITE NAME: THE WESTERN WALL, ALSO KNOWN AS THE KOTEL**

Include this on your tour? yes / no

**Why?** The Kotel is one of the most famous sites in Israel. People who are interested in history appreciate it for its archaeological significance; many connect to it religiously.

**SITE NAME:** _____

Include this on your tour? yes / no

**Why?**

_____

_____

_____

Note: Scan code or visit bhlink.me/israel9 to learn more about each site.

**SITE NAME:**

Include this on your tour? yes / no

**Why?**

**SITE NAME:**

Include this on your tour? yes / no

**Why?**

**SITE NAME:**

Include this on your tour? yes / no

**Why?**

Draw a  next to the site in Jerusalem that you would most want to visit.

# Tel Aviv

Some people say, "While Jerusalem prays, Tel Aviv plays." That's because while Jerusalem is full of historical and holy sites, Tel Aviv is the modern heart of the country. Situated on the Mediterranean coast, it's a huge beach town, with lots of sandy spots at which to surf, boat, swim, and play.

**SITE NAME:**

_____

Include this on your tour? yes / no

**Why?**

_____

_____

_____

**SITE NAME:**

_____

Include this on your tour? yes / no

**Why?**

_____

_____

_____

Draw a ☆ next to the site in Tel Aviv that you would most want to visit.

# The Best of the Rest

Exhilarating and diverse nature; amazing archaeological sites; modern, dynamic cities: The rest of the country has got it all. Packed with geographical diversity and cultural treasures, here are (just some of) the best of the rest of Israel:

**SITE NAME:**

Include this on your tour? yes / no

**Why?**

**SITE NAME:**

Include this on your tour? yes / no

**Why?**

**SITE NAME:**
_____

Include this on your tour? yes / no

**Why?**
_____

_____

_____

 **SITE NAME:**
_____

Include this on your tour? yes / no

**Why?**
_____

_____

_____

 **SITE NAME:**
_____

Include this on your tour? yes / no

**Why?**
_____

_____

_____

**SITE NAME:**

Include this on your tour? yes / no

**Why?**

**SITE NAME:**

Include this on your tour? yes / no

**Why?**

Draw a ⭐ next to the site from "The Best of the Rest" that you would most want to visit.

**Step 3:** Complete your recommended itinerary for your customer below.

Dear Client,

The themes for your upcoming trip to Israel will be: "Israel: It's ______________" (ancient / modern / natural / Jewish / fun/ other).

These are the top five places I suggest you visit, to tie in to your chosen theme(s):

1. ______________________________
2. ______________________________
3. ______________________________
4. ______________________________
5. ______________________________

I also recommend that you visit these sites:

A Jewish site: ______________________________

A historical site: ______________________________

A modern site: ______________________________

A cultural site: ______________________________

A nature site: ______________________________

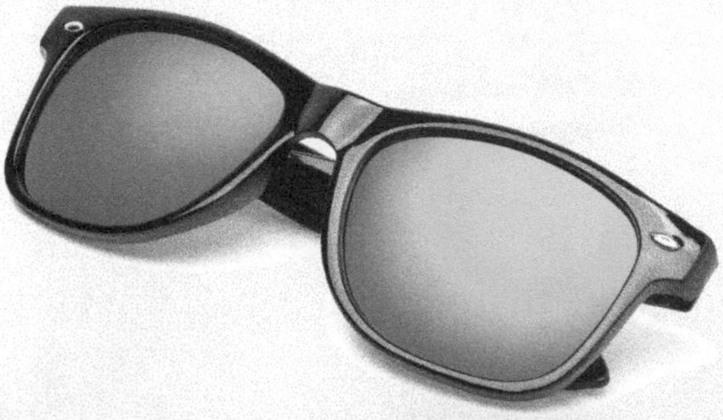

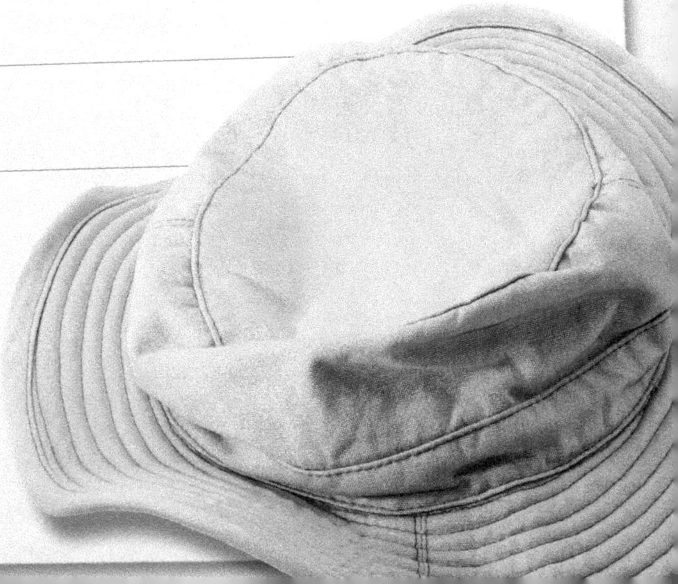

Share your itinerary with a friend, and discuss the following questions:

1. Why did you pick the activities that you did for your customers?

2. Which of the sites did you put stars next to? What about them was most appealing to you?

3. Which of the sites that your friend picked would you want to visit? Why?

# Plan Your Menu

If you were visiting Israel, where would you want to eat? Imagine that you and your friend are stopping for dinner in Tel Aviv. Visit bhlink.me/israel9 to see four different Tel Aviv restaurant menus.

Then, create your perfect meal by picking one dish from each of the menus: an appetizer, a main dish, a side dish, and a dessert.

## MENU

### APPETIZER

### MAIN DISH

### SIDE DISH

### DESSERT

- What countries or cultures do you think influenced the dishes that you chose for your meal?

- Which dish that you chose is the most "Israeli"? Why do you think so?

# It's Meaningful: Voluntourism in Israel

Many tourists come to Israel to have a great time and a meaningful experience. This type of tourism is called voluntourism.

*Yair and his brother Amir harvest potatoes for Leket Israel, Israel's National Food Bank. Leket rescues surplus crops in Israel and redistributes them to those who need it most.*

*Volunteers help a student at the Keren Or Jerusalem Center for Blind Children with Multiple Disabilities.*

# Making a Difference

In groups of two or three, choose a voluntourism project that you think you would want to participate in. Make a list of social justice issues that are important to you; for example, helping the elderly, taking care of the environment, visiting the sick. Then, in groups of two or three, discuss the questions below and select a voluntourism project in Israel in which you'd like to participate.

At Pantry Packers, located in Talpiot, Jerusalem, Kayla packs food for families in need.

1. Would you like to work with people or animals?

2. Would you prefer to do work that uses your mind (like creating something) or work that uses your body (like clearing a nature trail)?

3. What would you hope to learn from your experience?

4. What skills do you have to offer (for example, good with children, skilled at computers)?

| Volunteer project name and mission | Reasons you chose it |
|---|---|
| | |

Visit bhlink.me/israel9 for more resources on voluntourism opportunities in Israel.

# Talk about It!

1. Have you ever been to Israel? If you have, describe the most memorable experience you had there. If not, whom do you know who has visited? What have they told you about their experiences?

2. Whom do you know that might not enjoy a visit to Israel? Why do you think they wouldn't?

3. Whom do you know that you think would get the most out of a visit to Israel? Why do you think so?

## Conclusion

# What Does Israel Mean to Me?

## A Dream for Israel's Future

Imagine it is the year 2050. You are in Israel and want to send a message home that describes what the country and people are like.

What do you think will be the same as it is today? Different? What do you think will be more complicated? Less complicated?

Write your message here:

**New message**

To

Subject

Send  | +

# Design an Israeli Star

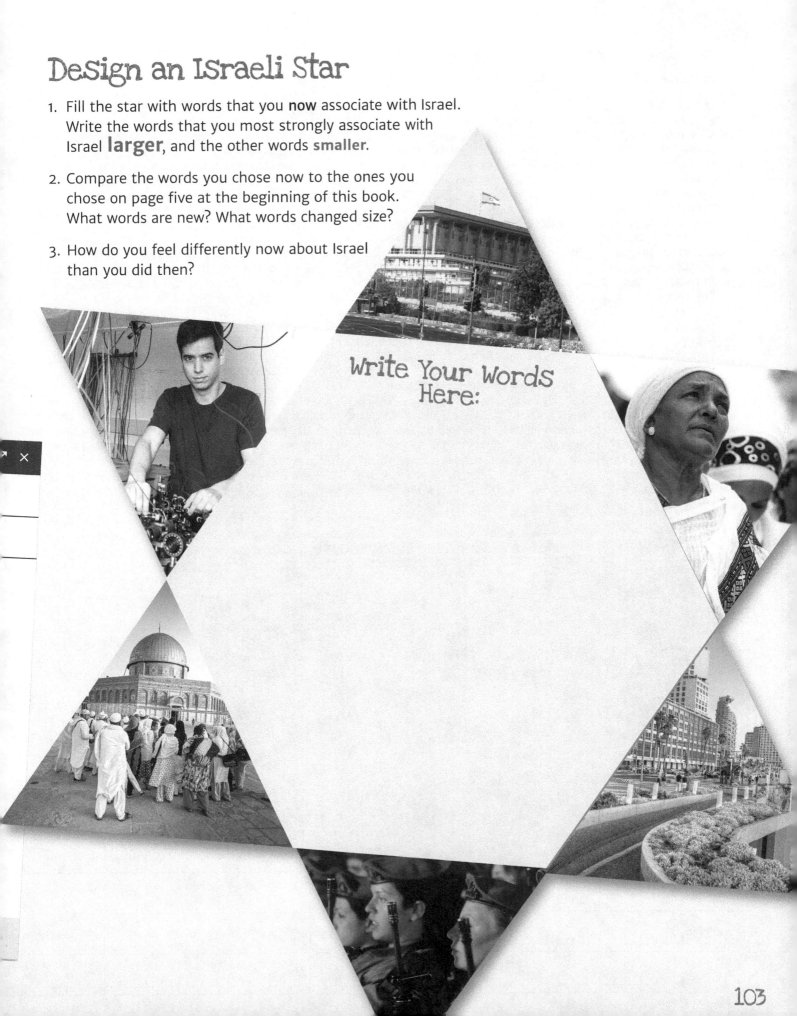

1. Fill the star with words that you **now** associate with Israel. Write the words that you most strongly associate with Israel **larger**, and the other words **smaller**.

2. Compare the words you chose now to the ones you chose on page five at the beginning of this book. What words are new? What words changed size?

3. How do you feel differently now about Israel than you did then?

Write Your Words Here:

The publisher gratefully acknowledges the following sources of images:

(B=bottom; T=top; L=left; R=right; M=middle)

**COVER:** SHUTTERSTOCK.COM: Front: ColorMaker T; Ryan Rodrick Beile B; ChameleonsEye R; dnaveh L. Back: ULKA-STUDIO T; illpaxphotomatic TL; Moving Moment B; JFragments (brick). WIKIMEDIA COMMONS: BL. **INTERIOR:** Jim McMahon 8; Kesselman/Maryles 11BM; Maccabeats and Abbie Sophia 13; Mark Koffsky 22M; Shevi Arnold 23T, 24T, 28BM, 31TR; Behrman House 24M, 30T, 31TL, 29 (Sox); Jeremy Koffsky 28BL, 28BR, 29TR, 46; Hand in Hand 32B, 33; Dan Nichols 37T; The Fountainheads 37M; Knesset website 43TL; Israel Sinai KKL-JNF Photo Archive 53BL; Creative Commons / Music in Common / US Embassy Jerusalem 62B; Andrew Neusner 68BL; American Technion Society / Cornell Tech Campus / IWAN BAAN 73B; Corali Gat / Noffar Gat 85B; Weizmann Institute of Science 86, 103; Ann Koffsky 92B; Dena Nesner 96M; Caryn Lenefsky 96B; Alison Gross and Sarah Weinberg 100TL; Keren Or Inc. 100B; Gaby Shine Markowitz 101T. GOVERNMENT PRESS OFFICE: Moshe Milner 19T, 29B; Haim Zach 28TL; Fritz Cohen 34TR; Avi Ohayon 45, 66TR; Zoltan Kluger 51; 52B; 52T; 54. SHUTTERSTOCK.COM: timurockart (by the #s); M-vector (WDYS); Happy Art (debate); tovovan(talk about it); Kapitosh (burst); Protasov AN 2; ULKASTUDIO 4L; Naeblys 4R; maratr 10T; ixpert 10BL; RnDmS 10BR; Viktoria Gavrilina 11BR, 103; Khirman Vladimir 12TL; Daniel Borgenicht 12TR; Inna Reznik 12BL; ChameleonsEye 14T, 18T, 22BL, 24B, 71T, 83M, 93T, 95T, 96T; subarashii21 14B, 16M, 46R; Jemastock 15T, 17T; Roman Yanushevsky 15B, 42; Nitr 17M; tristan tan 17BR; catwalker 17BL; Alexander Raths 18M; Boris-B 22T; Fat Jackey 22TM, 102T; illpaxphotomatic 22TL; StockStudio 22B; The World in HDR 24B, 94M; Vector Maniac 25BL; diplomedia 25BR; bonchan 26B; Firas Nashed 26T; DarioZg 28BL; nikolae 29TL; Mick Harper 29MR; cunaplus 30B; Zhukov 31MR; Robert Hoetink 35L; Kyrylo Glivin 35M; akturer 35R; Tanya Lapidus 36B; Ksusha Khomyakova 37B; hikrcn 38T; Bernhard Richter 38M; Daniel Reiner 38BL; Christos Georghiou 39TR; Din Mohd Yaman 41TL; Ryan Rodrick Beiler 41TM, 67B; glenda 41TR; pokku 44T; Magicleaf 46(hat); DnD-Production.com 53T; tomertu 53 BR; lev radin 60R; Jiri Hera 61T; Ryan Rodrick Beiler 62B; Brian Maudsley 67T; Lorna Wu 72T; KelseyJ 72BL; Albert H. Teich 72ML; Ben Gingell 72MR; a katz 77M, 79; Lucy 78; Soonthorn Wongsaita 80TR; kavring 80TL, cactus_camera 80BR; Kartinkin77 80BL; dolphfyn 80M; John Theodor 81; pro500 82, Yontsen 82-84, 92-97 (arrows), zilber42 83T, Andre Nery 83L, Mohd Syis Zulkipli 84TL, Phonlamai Photo 84TR, Jose HERNANDEZ Camera 51 86B, 92M; Tanis Saucier 87; Manaken2012 88TL; Mega Pixel 88T; Roman Samokhin 88TR; David Cohen 156 88M; studio evasion 89B; Protasov AN 90TR; Kyrylo Glivin 90TL; Cacheman 90B; Phovoir 91; JekLi 92T; Alexey Stiop 93M; Alexandre Rotenberg 93B; StockStudio 94T; alefbet 95M; Max Topchii 95M; Oleg Golovnev 95T; vvvita 97T; Shimon Bar 97M; LeonP 97B; Sangaroon 98BL; rizalfaridz7 98BR; Ivanna Grigorova 99TL; Anna_Pustynnikova 99BL; Moving Moment 99TR; Maxim Larin 99B; Boris-B 104. WIKIMEDIA COMMONS: 6; 7; 10BM; 11BL; 15M; 16T; 16B; 21; 22TR; 25T; 27T; 32T; 34TL; 36T; 36M; 38 BR; 43TR; 44T; 49T; 50; 52L; 52ML; 55-59; 60L; 63-65; 66TL; BL; TR; 68T; 73TR, TM, TL; 74TR; 75; 76; 77T; 77B; 82; 83B; 84 (logos); 85T; 94B; 103.

*Tel Aviv, Israel*

Printed in the USA
CPSIA information can be obtained
at www.ICGtesting.com
JSHW051327120824
67987JS00005B/326

9 780874 419825